Vol. XCVI

No. 1

SO-DLE-926

Adult
Bible Class

WINTER QUARTER   December 2009, January, February 2010

Editor in Chief: Beryl C. Bidlen

Edited and published quarterly by
THE INCORPORATED TRUSTEES OF THE
GOSPEL WORKER SOCIETY
UNION GOSPEL PRESS DIVISION

Rev. W. B. Musselman, Founder

Price: $2.25 per quarter
$9.00 per year

ISBN 978-1-934981-68-9

A UNION GOSPEL PRESS PUBLICATION • "CHRISTIAN LIFE SERIES"

Lessons based on International Sunday School Lessons; the International Bible Lessons
for Christian Teaching, copyright © 2006 by the Committee on the Uniform Series and used
with permission. Edited and published quarterly by The Incorporated Trustees of the Gospel
Worker Society, Union Gospel Press Division, 2000 Brookpark Road, Cleveland, Ohio
44109-5812. Mailing address: P.O. Box 6059, Cleveland, Ohio 44101-1059.

Reflections on Christ's Fulfillment

BY JOHN HAYNES

In his play *Wilhelm Tell,* Johann Christoph Friedrich von Schiller wrote, "Who reflects too much will accomplish little" (act III, scene 1).

The Bible is full of reflections. It was common for the Jews to rehearse their history, and one could be certain to buy time if needed by retelling Jewish history (cf. Acts 7:2-53). Yet since all of Scripture is God breathed, we must realize that all such reflections are indeed God's will. Amid these reflections, it is apparent that God has accomplished much!

This quarter we will study how Christ is the fulfillment of all that God intended. A fulfillment can be thought of as a type of accomplishment. We will see how Jesus fulfilled God's will in many different ways.

In our first lesson, we will see how Jesus was the fulfillment of the Davidic kingdom because His genealogical line proved that He was a son of David. Since the Romans destroyed the temple in A.D. 70, along with all the genealogical records, no one since that time could claim David as an ancestor; but the book of Matthew clearly shows the link between David and Christ.

Lesson 2 gives us a foreshadowing of the Messiah's birth. The book of Isaiah has been called the Gospel of the Old Testament, and with good reason. Chapter 7 contains a prophecy about how Jesus would be born of a virgin, an event that never happened before or since.

Lesson 3 reminds us of the birth of God's Son, our Saviour. Since Jesus was and is fully God and since He became a man at His incarnation, He can truly be called "Immanuel."

Lesson 4 gives us further confirmation of who Jesus was when He came into this world. The wise men came to visit Him, knowing that He was the King of the Jews. How they knew this we do not know, but obviously God had revealed it to them. The fact that they worshiped Jesus also shows that they recognized Him as God. Joseph and Mary did too, or they would have been aghast at such genuflection.

Jesus was baptized by John in the Jordan, and some have tried to state that it was at that moment that Jesus became divine. Lesson 5 will show that nothing could be further from the truth. He was the Son of God before time began. He will be the Son of God after the world ends and Satan is cast into the Lake of Fire (Rev. 20:10).

We all face temptation every day, many times a day. As lesson 6 tells us, Jesus was tempted too. That should encourage us because it shows that He faced what we face. The difference in His temptations is that He withstood each with flying colors. How did He do this? He quoted Scripture. It seems that knowing God's Word really does keep us from sin (Ps. 119:11).

Have you ever wished that you could perform some miracle to show others that your faith is real? Sadly, many charlatans who do claim to perform miracles actually take away from the gospel. Yes, Jesus did many miracles to attest to His identity as the Messiah (lesson 7), but that is not what we are called to do. We are called to testify that Jesus is the Messiah and the Sav-

young man. Their rejection was typical of many.

We know that Jesus came to "seek and to save that which was lost" (Luke 19:10). That included Gentiles as well as Jews. Lesson 10 shows how a Canaanite woman believed in Him and would not leave until He healed her daughter. This Gentile woman had more faith than many Jews.

When Jesus asked His disciples who they thought He was, Peter answered in no uncertain terms that He was "the Christ, the Son of the living God" (Matt. 16:16). Jesus pointed out that God the Father had led him to say that. In lesson 11, we will see what else Peter said and how Jesus dealt with it.

Jesus' transfiguration and conversation with Moses and Elijah is one of the stranger incidents in His earthly life; yet as we see in lesson 12, it showed His disciples once again that God was His Father. There could be no mistake that the voice was from heaven. By seeing this miracle, they could testify of their firsthand knowledge of Jesus' divinity.

When Mary, the sister of Martha and Lazarus, anointed Jesus with a very expensive perfume, Jesus made it clear that she had done so as a precursor to His burial. Lesson 13 indicates she came under fire for supposedly wasting such expensive oil, but in Jesus' view, she knew better than even His disciples what awaited Him very soon.

Our lessons this quarter, as always, are compelling. They are compelling because the Word of God is compelling. Even when we study a passage over again (might we say we reflect?), we can learn new things because the Word of God comes directly from Him. "From God's lips to my ears," we could say. Yes, Jesus fulfilled the complete plan of God for us.

iour of all mankind.

We all know that prayer is important; we also know that we do not pray as often as we should. One reason that may be is that we think of prayer as a chore, but Jesus made it clear that in coming to Him, He will give us rest for our souls (lesson 8). He delights in hearing our sorrows. He wants to bear our labors. We can be encouraged by this because it is clear that He is doing all the work. He is truly a Friend like no other!

No one likes to be rejected. Most of us have been rejected at some point in our lives. Jesus knows what that is like. No one ever suffered rejection like Him. Of course we know that He was rejected in His crucifixion, but lesson 9 deals with rejection by those He had grown up with in Nazareth. They of all people should have seen who He really was. He had never sinned as a boy or a

Scripture Lesson Text

RUTH 4:13 So Bo′az took Ruth, and she was his wife: and when he went in unto her, the LORD gave her conception, and she bare a son.

14 And the women said unto Na-o′mi, Blessed *be* the LORD, which hath not left thee this day without a kinsman, that his name may be famous in Is′ra-el.

15 And he shall be unto thee a restorer of *thy* life, and a nourisher of thine old age: for thy daughter in law, which loveth thee, which is better to thee than seven sons, hath born him.

16 And Na-o′mi took the child, and laid it in her bosom, and became nurse unto it.

17 And the women her neighbours gave it a name, saying, There is a son born to Na-o′mi; and they called his name O′bed: he *is* the father of Jes′se, the father of Da′vid.

MATT. 1:1 The book of the generation of Je′sus Christ, the son of Da′vid, the son of A′bra-ham.

2 A′bra-ham begat I′saac; and I′saac begat Ja′cob; and Ja′cob begat Ju′das and his brethren;

3 And Ju′das begat Pha′res and Za′ra of Tha′mar; and Pha′res begat Es′rom; and Es′rom begat A′ram;

4 And A′ram begat A-min′a-dab; and A-min′a-dab begat Na-as′son; and Na-as′son begat Sal′mon;

5 And Sal′mon begat Bo′oz of Ra′chab; and Bo′oz begat O′bed of Ruth; and O′bed begat Jes′se;

6 And Jes′se begat Da′vid the king; and Da′vid the king begat Sol′o-mon of her *that had been the wife* of U-ri′as.

4

The Lineage of David

Lesson: Ruth 4:13-17; Matthew 1:1-6

Read: Ruth 4:13-17; Matthew 1:1-17

TIMES: about 1120 B.C.; A.D. 50   PLACES: Bethlehem; unknown

GOLDEN TEXT—"The women her neighbours gave it a name, saying, There is a son born to Naomi; and they called his name Obed: he is the father of Jesse, the father of David" (Ruth 4:17).

Lesson Exposition

A SIMPLE BIRTH—Ruth 4:13-17

Birth of a son (Ruth 4:13). The book of Ruth gives us one of the greatest love stories in the Bible. You will remember that Elimelech took Naomi, his wife, and his two sons to Moab during a time of famine in Bethlehem. Over a period of time, both Elimelech and his sons died, leaving two daughters-in-law with Naomi. When she heard that the famine was over, she decided to return home. One daughter-in-law did as Naomi suggested and stayed with her family in Moab. The other, Ruth, went to Bethlehem with her.

Ruth soon proved herself to be a loyal family member, willing to do her part in providing for herself and Naomi. Upon leaving home to find a place where she could glean grain, she was providentially led to the fields of Boaz.

At some point, Naomi decided upon a course of action that would provide Ruth with a new husband and future security. Following the customs of their culture, Ruth, under Naomi's guidance, let it be known to Boaz that she would like him to be her protector and provider (Ruth 3). Her actions were in essence a request for him to take her as his wife. Again following the customs of the culture, Boaz negotiated with a closer relative and was given the freedom to marry Ruth and redeem her property (4:1-12).

That brings us to the statement of Ruth 4:13: "So Boaz took Ruth, and she was his wife: and when he went in unto her, the Lord gave her conception, and she bare a son." This was surely the Lord at work. Ruth had been childless during her previous marriage, but now "the Lord gave her conception."

Praise by the women (Ruth 4:14-15). When Naomi arrived in Bethlehem from Moab, she caused quite a stir among the people (1:19). Evidently, she and her husband had been popular and very well respected by the populace. Apparently, she had changed in appearance, for the women kept asking whether she was really Naomi.

It was those women who now expressed joy for Naomi in the birth of her grandson. They had seen her emptiness and bitterness when she returned from Moab, and now they saw her joy and fulfillment. Their praise was over the fact that the Lord had given Naomi a kinsman, referring to Ruth's baby, who was her heir. Their prayer for him was threefold: that he would be famous in Israel; that he would give new life to Naomi; and that he would be effective in caring for her through her old age.

For the women to wish Naomi's grandson to be a restorer of Naomi's life probably points to their understanding that the loss of her husband and sons had left Naomi empty. Life had turned into hardship, and from a human perspective she had little left to live for. The women wanted this new baby to become a means of changing that. In fact, until this birth, Naomi had no hope for the continuation of her family line.

Every Jewish woman wanted to give birth to a son, always with the accompanying deep hope that maybe he would be the promised Messiah. To have seven sons was considered to be an indication of great blessing from the Lord. In giving Naomi a grandson and in loving her selflessly, Ruth had already proved herself to be worth more than seven sons.

Nursed by Naomi (Ruth 4:16-17). There are those who believe that when Naomi took the child and laid him on her bosom, she was performing some kind of formal act of adoption. We do not see evidence for this in the context. Her actions were probably nothing more than those of a happy grandmother. She became a nurse to the baby in the sense of a guardian, or a nanny. The Hebrew word is not a definite indication of her being a wet nurse. Naomi is simply seen as a loving, doting grandmother.

The word translated "son" in Ruth 4:17 can refer to any male descendant. The baby did not officially become Naomi's son, but he was indeed her grandson and a legitimate member of the family line. There is no explanation as to why the neighbor women named him instead of the immediate family, but they chose to call him "Obed," which means "servant."

We instantly become aware of the magnitude of this birth when we read that Obed became the father of Jesse, who was the father of David. This is the first mention of David in the Bible; so up to this point in Israel's history, there was nothing to indicate how significant David would be. Since we have what is recorded in the books of Samuel and following, especially the giving of the Davidic covenant, we have a fuller understanding than did those in Boaz and Ruth's day of how great this birth truly was.

A SIGNIFICANT GENEALOGY— Matt. 1:1-6

The original fathers (Matt. 1:1-2). It had been over four hundred years since Israel's last prophets had spoken. Still, many in Israel were faithfully looking for the appearance of the promised Messiah. Matthew's purpose in writing his Gospel was to prove to the Jews that Jesus of Nazareth was that promised One.

Matthew's opening sentence was therefore an attention grabber, meant to get his readers thinking about the Person of Jesus. It immediately connected Him to two of the greatest covenants God had given to Israel—namely, the Abrahamic (Gen. 12; 15) and the Davidic (II Sam. 7). The Jews would then have wanted to know, Does His genealogy follow through and make Him the legal heir to the throne of David? If so, this surely was the promised Messiah. The genealogy given in Matthew traces Him through Joseph, His legal father (1:16).

The first four names Matthew gave are well documented in the book of Genesis. Here we read of Abraham and the long-awaited birth of Isaac from the aged Sarah (21:1-7). Isaac then had to appeal to God on behalf of his wife, Rebekah, who gave birth to Jacob and Esau (25:19-26). From Jacob came twelve sons, who were the foundation of the tribes of the nation of Israel. Through various events, Reuben, Simeon, and Levi lost the right of being primary heir to Jacob. Judah was next in line and is listed in Matthew 1:2 as the family leader.

In Jacob's final words to his sons, he

pointed Judah out as the one through whom the ultimate ruler of Israel would come (Gen. 49:10). Even though he too had been involved in sinful activity (chap. 38), he had subsequently lived in a way that qualified him to lead.

The middle generations (Matt. 1:3-4). It is most unusual for women to be named in biblical genealogies and even more unusual for one with a tainted background. Tamar is the first of four women mentioned in Matthew's genealogy. Judah had thought she was a prostitute and slept with her (Gen. 38:13-16). As a result, she gave birth to twins, Pharez and Zarah (vss. 27-30). God truly does work in ways beyond our comprehension, for we would probably have gone out of our way to avoid including such an individual in a line as important as this one.

No doubt we are seeing the mercy and grace of God in operation. The other three women were also questionable. Ruth was a Gentile, Rahab was a Gentile and a prostitute, and Bath-sheba was involved in adultery. Although Judah never married Tamar as far as we can tell ("he knew her again no more" according to Genesis 38:26), it was through his son Pharez that the genealogical line led to the Messiah. We cannot help seeing that God in His goodness graciously reaches out to and desires to use all who are willing to do His will.

"Matthew's inclusion of four particular women in his genealogy reveals his concern to do more than relay historical data. . . . These women were less-than-sterling examples to have in one's ancestral line. . . . The suspicion of illegitimacy surrounded these four; . . . this fits with the suspicion surrounding Mary, Jesus' mother. . . . These were normal people, sometimes caught up in their own sin, all of them in need of God's mercy and grace." (Osborne and Comfort, eds., *Life Application Bible Commentary,* Tyndale).

The line to David (Matt. 1:5-6). In these verses two of the other three women are named, and the other is mentioned.

Detailed study of biblical genealogies will lead to the conclusion that not every person in the line is mentioned in the text. While there are unanswered questions about this genealogy, Matthew's point is clear. The line to the Messiah includes the patriarch Abraham and King David.

—*Keith E. Eggert.*

QUESTIONS

1. What is significant about the book of Ruth?
2. What is unique about Ruth's inclusion in the genealogy that leads to the Messiah?
3. Why were Naomi's friends so excited about Ruth's baby?
4. What threefold prayer did they make for Obed?
5. How did Naomi reveal her acceptance and joy over Obed's birth?
6. Why was the birth of Ruth's son emphasized so much at the end of the book?
7. How did Matthew get the attention of his Jewish readers at the beginning of his Gospel, and why was this information important?
8. What is unusual about Judah being listed after his father, Jacob, in this genealogy?
9. What is unique about Pharez being in Christ's genealogy?
10. Who were the women included in this genealogy, and what might this reveal about God's choices?

—*Keith E. Eggert.*

PRACTICAL POINTS

1. Marriage is the permanent, faithful union of a man and a woman to produce godly children (Ruth 4:13).
2. Childbearing is a blessing and a joy, bringing honor and celebration to the community (vs. 14).
3. Motherhood offers comfort in old age and hope to future generations (vss. 15-16).
4. Each child is another instrument for God to accomplish His purpose for creation (vs. 17).
5. Christ's genealogy is universal—no race or station is excluded from His grace (Matt. 1:1-6).
6. God used a diverse mixture of human sinners to bring forth His perfect Saviour (Matt. 1:1-6).

—John M. Lody.

RESEARCH AND DISCUSSION

1. Discuss God's original design and purpose for marriage and how ideas in modern society have perverted His intentions.
2. Do you view childbearing as a joyful blessing? Discuss how many modern attitudes have tended to spoil our feelings about having children. Have Christians bought into these attitudes?
3. Examine the types of people who make up the genealogy of Christ in Matthew 1. Did God choose these people because of their own righteousness or because of His desire to use them, regardless of who they were? What impact does your answer have on your view of salvation today?

—John M. Lody.

Golden Text Illuminated

"The women her neighbours gave it a name, saying, There is a son born to Naomi; and they called his name Obed: he is the father of Jesse, the father of David" (Ruth 4:17).

Besides revealing valuable genealogical data, the golden text also reflects a rare way of giving a child a name. Usually the parents give a child his name. However, Ruth 4:17 says that female neighbors gave Ruth's son the name "Obed." Boaz and Ruth accepted this name for their child.

That these women so boldly expressed their desire for the child to be named "Obed" probably shows how impressed they were with the loving-kindness and providential care of God, which had been displayed in the lives of Naomi, Ruth, and Boaz. The name "Obed," which means "one who serves," most likely describes the feelings of the women. They longed for the child to grow up to serve God.

When we compare the golden text, which comes at the end of the book of Ruth, with the first chapter of Ruth, we observe a great contrast. In chapter 1, we see overwhelming grief and bitterness of soul after Naomi's husband and her two sons died prematurely.

In Ruth 4, however, we observe a drastically different scene. Naomi's bitterness has been replaced with indescribable joy. She rejoiced in Boaz, God's unexpected provider for her old age and the husband of Ruth, her daughter-in-law.

These contrasting scenes of misery and bliss remind us of the fall of Adam and redemption in Christ (Eph. 1:7; I Pet. 1:8-9).

—Karl Kloppmann.

Scripture Lesson Text

ISA. 7:13 And he said, Hear ye now, O house of Da'vid; *Is it* a small thing for you to weary men, but will ye weary my God also?

14 Therefore the Lord himself shall give you a sign; Behold, a virgin shall conceive, and bear a son, and shall call his name Im-man'u-el.

15 Butter and honey shall he eat, that he may know to refuse the evil, and choose the good.

16 For before the child shall know to refuse the evil, and choose the good, the land that thou abhorrest shall be forsaken of both her kings.

17 The Lᴏʀᴅ shall bring upon thee, and upon thy people, and upon thy father's house, days that have not come, from the day that E'phra-im departed from Ju'dah; *even* the king of As-syr'i-a.

LUKE 1:30 And the angel said unto her, Fear not, Ma'ry: for thou hast found favour with God.

31 And, behold, thou shalt conceive in thy womb, and bring forth a son, and shalt call his name JE'SUS.

32 He shall be great, and shall be called the Son of the Highest: and the Lord God shall give unto him the throne of his father Da'vid:

33 And he shall reign over the house of Ja'cob for ever; and of his kingdom there shall be no end.

34 Then said Ma'ry unto the angel, How shall this be, seeing I know not a man?

35 And the angel answered and said unto her, The Ho'ly Ghost shall come upon thee, and the power of the Highest shall overshadow thee: therefore also that holy thing which shall be born of thee shall be called the Son of God.

36 And, behold, thy cousin E-lis'a-beth, she hath also conceived a son in her old age: and this is the sixth month with her, who was called barren.

37 For with God nothing shall be impossible.

38 And Ma'ry said, Behold the handmaid of the Lord; be it unto me according to thy word. And the angel departed from her.

The Foreshadowing of Messiah's Birth

Lesson: Isaiah 7:13-17; Luke 1:30-38

Read: Isaiah 7:13-17; Luke 1:26-38

TIMES: about 734 B.C.; 6 or 5 B.C.   PLACES: Jerusalem; Nazareth

---

GOLDEN TEXT—"The Lord himself shall give you a sign; Behold, a virgin shall conceive, and bear a son, and shall call his name Immanuel" (Isaiah 7:14).

Lesson Exposition

A PROPHECY THROUGH ISAIAH— Isa. 7:13-17

A sign coming (Isa. 7:13-14). The Lord spoke very firmly to Ahaz through the Prophet Isaiah. In order to completely allay Ahaz's fears, God told him to ask for a sign confirming His word (vss. 10-11). But Ahaz arrogantly refused. Was it his unbelief in God, his annoyance at being told what to do by Isaiah, or simply his overwhelming pride that he felt no need for a confirmed word from God? Whatever his reason, Ahaz couched his refusal in the excuse of not wanting to test God, which was no doubt a transparently hypocritical response!

A comparison with II Kings 16:7 reveals that Ahaz was seeking assistance from the king of Assyria; so he apparently had no intention of relying on God for deliverance. In response to Ahaz's refusal of Isaiah's command to ask (Isaiah 7:11, which is in the imperative in the Hebrew), the Lord spoke to both Ahaz and other people: "Hear ye now, O house of David; Is it a small thing for you to weary men, but will ye weary my God also?" (vs. 13). Isaiah said "my God" because Ahaz had already refused to listen to Him and could not claim Him as his God.

That did not stop God from giving a sign. The sign would be the birth of a son through a virgin, and he was to be named "Immanuel." We know from Matthew 1:22-23 that this is a prophecy about the coming of the Messiah, which was fulfilled in the birth of Jesus. A question then naturally arises. How was this promised birth a sign to Ahaz that he could trust God's word about not needing to worry over the alliance of Rezin and Pekah? The answer is that it is common for prophetic utterances to have both near and far fulfillments.

We need to understand that the Greek word translated "virgin" in Matthew 1:23 can mean nothing other than a woman who has not had sexual experience. Mary fulfilled this prophecy in her pregnancy. The Hebrew word translated "virgin" in Isaiah 7:14, however, is not so definite. The word 'almah means "lass," or "maiden." There is a masculine counterpart that means "lad." It is different from the word bethulah, which is the normal word for a virgin.

In this case the virgin was probably a young woman of marriageable age who could become betrothed at any time. In order for the sign to have meaning for Ahaz, this young woman had to be someone he knew; Isaiah did not include that information, perhaps because the more important message was the ultimate fulfillment in the Messiah.

A change coming (Isa. 7:15-16). If we think the previous verse was difficult to understand, we might be surprised to know that these verses are equally difficult! First, the Hebrew word translated "butter" refers to milk that has curdled rather than that which has been churned into the kind of butter we know. For this reason we read the word "curds" in several Bible translations and in many commentaries. A diet of curds and honey was one that became necessary in hard times.

The baby to be born would be present in these difficult days that were coming. The two things that are mentioned as part of this sign to Ahaz are the time after the child would be weaned and able to eat food and the time when he would be old enough to know right from wrong. Isaiah's message was that by the time these two things were true of this baby, God would have already dealt with the two kings coming against Ahaz.

Isaiah 8:3-4 seems to speak of the same time. Isaiah's wife would also have a baby, calling him Maher-shalal-hash-baz. This was a symbolic name meaning "speed to the spoil and hasten to the booty," a description of what Assyria would do when it attacked Israel and Syria. That would happen before Isaiah's baby was old enough to begin talking.

A captivity coming (Isa. 7:17). That should have sounded like good news to Ahaz, but there was bad news at the same time. Assyria would indeed destroy Syria and Israel, but she would then attack Judah. God was behind this movement because of Judah's wickedness. This particular attack was going to be the worst since the nation split. The name "Ephraim" is used here to refer to the northern nation of Israel because Ephraim had become the dominant tribe of that nation.

A PROPHECY THROUGH GABRIEL—Luke 1:30-38

An announcement (Luke 1:30-31). It was a startling moment for young Mary. An angel suddenly walked into her presence and greeted her: "Hail, thou that art highly favoured, the Lord is with thee: blessed art thou among women" (vs. 28). As would anyone, Mary felt confused over such a greeting, wondering what the angel could possibly mean. His announcement was very similar to what he had said earlier to Zacharias (vs. 13)—namely, that she did not need to be afraid and that she was going to have a son.

As with Zacharias, Mary was to name the boy what the angel told her. Zacharias had been told he did not need to fear because his prayers had been heard by God. Mary did not need to fear because she had found favor with God.

An exaltation (Luke 1:32-33). The angel made five significant statements about Mary's son. First, He would be great. The Greek word here is *megas.* Jesus would certainly be no ordinary baby, for He was superior to all. Second, Mary's son would be known as "the Son of the Highest."

Third, Mary was told that God was going to put her son on the throne of David. Being the godly young woman she was, Mary probably recognized that the angel spoke of the fulfillment of the Davidic covenant, which had been given nearly a thousand years earlier: "And thine house and thy kingdom shall be established for ever before thee: thy throne shall be established for ever" (II Sam. 7:16). Fourth, He would reign over the house of Jacob forever. This will begin in the millennium and continue right into eternity.

Fifth, adding certainty to the previous statement, Gabriel said her son's kingdom would never end. This will include far more than the house of Jacob. Just as God promised Abraham that he and his descendants were to be a blessing to the whole world, so Mary's son will reign over the entire universe.

An explanation (Luke 1:34-35). In spite of the fact that this was an unbelievably wonderful message, Mary had one question to be answered before she could fully accept and begin to look forward to this birth. God has established a physical means for children to be conceived and born, and so far she had not been married or had a sexual relationship with anyone. Furthermore, she had no intention of being immoral. She was planning to stay pure until her marriage to Joseph. How, then, could she become pregnant and give birth?

Gabriel's answer was that God was going to accomplish this through a miraculous conception. She would conceive through the power of the Holy Spirit and give birth while she was still a virgin. This creative act of the Spirit was necessary because of Jesus' pre-existence and deity. He already was and would continue to be the holy Son of God.

An example (Luke 1:36-38). In order to strengthen Mary's faith even further, Gabriel told her about her relative Elisabeth. Zacharias and Elisabeth were childless, and "both were now well stricken in years" (vs. 7). Gabriel had announced to Zacharias the coming birth of their son John, and as soon as the period of his temple service was completed, he returned home. Shortly after that his wife Elisabeth conceived (vss. 23-24).

Gabriel emphasized that Elisabeth had conceived in her old age even though she had been childless her entire life. He also informed Mary that Elisabeth was now in her sixth month of pregnancy; so she was well on her way to giving birth. If there were any doubts lingering in Mary's mind, this should answer them. However, to put a final conclusive thought in Mary's mind about the greatness and the possibility of this miracle, Gabriel reminded her that nothing is impossible with God.

In a moment of complete surrender and submission to God's will, Mary simply stated, "Behold the handmaid of the Lord; be it unto me according to thy word" (Luke 1:38). Can there be any better example in Scripture of willingness to do exactly what God wants?
—Keith E. Eggert.

QUESTIONS

1. Why was King Ahaz not seeking God's help against Israel and Syria?

2. How did Isaiah chide Ahaz when he refused to obey God's command for him to ask for a sign?

3. What was the sign God gave to Ahaz and the people?

4. What was the ultimate fulfillment of this prophecy, and how would the prophecy be a sign to Ahaz during his day?

5. What did Isaiah say was coming in the future for Judah?

6. How did Gabriel's appearances to Zacharias and to Mary compare?

7. What were some of the significant statements given to Mary about the son she would give birth to?

8. What specific covenant would she realize was being fulfilled?

9. What explanation and example did Gabriel give Mary to help her?

10. How did Mary respond to Gabriel's words?
—Keith E. Eggert.

PRACTICAL POINTS

1. It is dangerous enough to try the patience of people; how much more deadly is it to try the patience of almighty God (Isa. 7:13)?
2. Jesus is God come as man—God on our side. Once we are His, He is ours forever (vs. 14).
3. Jesus' perfect knowledge of good and evil makes Him the perfect judge of all (vss. 15-17).
4. God favored Mary as He does us, not for our own righteousness, but sovereignly, out of His mercy and grace (Luke 1:30-35).
5. "Impossible" is God's specialty; never count Him out (vss. 36-37)!
6. Mary's humility is not false; it is the only response to God for a favored sinner (vs. 38).

—John M. Lody.

RESEARCH AND DISCUSSION

1. How do people try the patience of God? What are the dangers for non-Christians? For Christians? Discuss ways to avoid trifling with God in your life.
2. We know "Immanuel" means "God with us"; but what does this name mean to us as Christians? Discuss Jesus' presence in your life and in the church as God's chosen people and what it signifies today.
3. Discuss the implications of Luke 1:37 for daily Christian living. How does God's power to do impossible things impact your life?
4. Discuss the virtues of humility. Should it be hard to be humble?

—John M. Lody.

Golden Text Illuminated

"The Lord himself shall give you a sign; Behold, a virgin shall conceive, and bear a son, and shall call his name Immanuel" (Isaiah 7:14).

In Isaiah 7:1-9 we read that God promised Ahaz, king of Judah, that the plan of the king of Israel and the king of Syria to attack Jerusalem and establish a new king would not come about. To overcome Ahaz's fear, God offered to give him a sign that the two kings would fall. Ahaz refused, but the Lord graciously gave him a sign despite his reluctance.

Ahaz was told, "A virgin shall conceive, and bear a son, and shall call his name Immanuel." The Hebrew word translated "virgin" is 'alma. That it meant "virgin" can be seen by the word the Septuagint translators (Jewish scholars who translated the Old Testament into Greek about 250 B.C.) chose to translate 'alma. They chose *parthenos,* which can only mean "virgin."

Literally, the golden text reads "the virgin," referring to a virgin who was well-known to Ahaz. Her child is referred to in Isaiah 7:15-16. Before he reached the age of moral discernment, the two kings Ahaz feared would be destroyed.

In Matthew 1:23 we read, "Behold, [the] virgin shall be with child, and shall bring forth a son, and they shall call his name Emmanuel." Matthew states that this prophecy was fulfilled in the birth of Jesus. The virgin in Ahaz's day conceived in a natural way. The virgin in Matthew's day conceived in a supernatural way without the aid of a man (1:18).

—Karl Kloppmann.

Scripture Lesson Text

MATT. 1:18 Now the birth of Je'sus Christ was on this wise: When as his mother Ma'ry was espoused to Jo'seph, before they came together, she was found with child of the Ho'ly Ghost.

19 Then Jo'seph her husband, being a just *man,* and not willing to make her a publick example, was minded to put her away privily.

20 But while he thought on these things, behold, the angel of the Lord appeared unto him in a dream, saying, Jo'seph, thou son of Da'vid, fear not to take unto thee Ma'ry thy wife: for that which is conceived in her is of the Ho'ly Ghost.

21 And she shall bring forth a son, and thou shalt call his name JE'SUS: for he shall save his people from their sins.

22 Now all this was done, that it might be fulfilled which was spoken of the Lord by the prophet, saying,

23 Behold, a virgin shall be with child, and shall bring forth a son, and they shall call his name Em-man'u-el, which being interpreted is, God with us.

24 Then Jo'seph being raised from sleep did as the angel of the Lord had bidden him, and took unto him his wife:

25 And knew her not till she had brought forth her firstborn son: and he called his name JE'SUS.

Emmanuel's Birth

(Christmas)

Lesson: Matthew 1:18-25

Read: Matthew 1:18-25

TIME: 6 or 5 B.C.   PLACE: Nazareth

GOLDEN TEXT—"She shall bring forth a son, and thou shalt call his name JESUS: for he shall save his people from their sins" (Matthew 1:21).

Lesson Exposition

TAUGHT BY GOD—Matt. 1:18-21

Joseph undecided (Matt. 1:18-19). In order to comprehend the element of shock that Joseph was about to experience, we need to remember what Jewish marriages were like. There were actually three stages that were part of the process of marriage. Unlike our modern-day practices, in which we date someone, fall in love, and then become engaged to marry, in New Testament days it was the parents who made the arrangements for their children. This still takes place in some cultures of the world.

The agreement made between the two sets of parents was sometimes reached several years before their children reached marrying age. In most of those cases, the children had no voice in the matter but simply had to accept their parents' decision. They might have lived for many years, therefore, before the second phase of the marriage process. This consisted of a formal, public ratification of the agreement in front of witnesses. This did not mean the young people lived together yet, but they were considered betrothed.

Betrothal was similar to what we call engagement, although betrothal was more binding than engagement. Betrothal, in fact, could not be broken except through death or divorce. The normal length of a betrothal was about a year, and during that time the couple continued to live at home with their families. This was enough time to prove the purity of the woman. Should she be found pregnant during this period, the betrothal could be annulled by a divorce process. Joseph and Mary were in this phase of their relationship.

The consummation of the marriage would occur when the bridegroom went to the home of the bride and took her to his home in a celebratory procession. The parable of the ten virgins in Matthew 25:1-13 illustrates this. In the meantime, the bridegroom was busy preparing a place for his bride.

It was during the betrothal time that Mary became pregnant through a miracle accomplished by the Holy Spirit of God. This left Joseph with a real dilemma. For all he knew, she had been unfaithful to him. If he stayed with her, the implication would be that he was the one who had been immoral with her. He had no desire for revenge, however, because he was a godly man. He was therefore giving careful thought to a private divorce that was simply a cultural matter of dismissing her from the relationship.

Joseph instructed (Matt. 1:20-21). We get so used to reading these descriptions of Jesus' birth that we sometimes forget that those involved were real people with the same emotions that we experience. Imagine, for example, how stunned and deeply disappointed Joseph must have felt when he heard about Mary's condition.

We are not told how long Joseph wrestled with his emotions, trying to decide his next action. We can be quite confident, however, that it was a very sad time for him. Perhaps it was as he was reaching his decision that the angel of the Lord appeared to him in a dream. We have to admire Joseph for the mature way he faced the situation. Instead of acting on his emotions, he took time to deliberate about what was the best course of action to take. This shows an element of spiritual maturity in him.

Because Joseph knew how to wait upon God for direction, he was able to hear when God spoke to him. In this case the message came through a dream. He was told he did not need to be fearful about taking Mary as his wife. There had been no immorality, for the baby she carried was the miraculous work of God's Holy Spirit. She would give birth to a son who was to be named "Jesus," meaning "Yahweh is salvation." He would be the One through whom people could be saved from their sins and thus be able to go to heaven.

The genealogy of Jesus given in Matthew 1:1-16 leads directly to Joseph, who is referred to as "Joseph the husband of Mary, of whom was born Jesus." The word "begat" is not used here as it is with every other birth in the list. It is clear from this wording that Joseph was not the physical father of Jesus. Because he was the husband of Mary, however, the birth of Jesus was kept in the royal and legal Davidic line.

"Why is the virgin birth important to the Christian faith? Jesus Christ, God's Son, had to be free from the sinful nature passed on to all other human beings by Adam. Because Jesus was born of a woman, He was a human being; but as the Son of God, Jesus was born without any trace of human sin. Jesus is both fully human and fully divine. The infinite, unlimited God took on the limitations of humanity so He could live and die for the salvation of all who believe in Him" (Osborne and Comfort, eds., *Life Application Bible Commentary,* Tyndale).

OBEDIENT TO GOD—Matt. 1:22-25

Prophecy being fulfilled (Matt. 1:22-23). Matthew wrote his Gospel specifically to explain to his fellow Jews that Jesus was the promised Messiah foretold in the Old Testament and the King of Israel. Because of this, he included many quotations of Old Testament statements. His explanation of Jesus' birth was done so that his readers could see the fulfillment of prophecy in it. This quotation is the first of many and is found in Isaiah 7:14.

The statement given in Matthew 1:23 was originally made to King Ahaz, but it had its ultimate fulfillment in the birth of Jesus (see last week's lesson). The name "Emmanuel," which means "God with us," speaks clearly of the combination of human and divine that is Jesus. It was God Himself who, in the Person of Jesus Christ, was going to dwell among His people. This leads to the obvious conclusion that Jesus is God. This human was also divine. The name also describes His role among people. As God in the flesh, He had come to save them.

In His humanity, Jesus experienced all the same needs we do. He got hungry and needed to eat (Matt. 4:2; 21:18). He got thirsty and needed to drink (John 19:28). He got tired and needed to sleep (Matt. 8:24). He became sad and heavy in spirit (23:37). He experienced anger toward people around Him (Mark 3:5). Is it not encouraging to us to know we have a Saviour who so fully understands all that we go through? This is why we find mercy and grace to help us when we experience times of need, both physical and spiritual.

While it is encouraging to us to realize His humanity and therefore His ability to identify with us in our needs, we must never forget Jesus' deity. Just as it is terribly disrespectful to refer to God as "the Man upstairs," so it is equally disrespectful to think of Jesus as no more than our "buddy." He is God and deserves our utmost respect.

Instruction being followed (Matt. 1:24-25). Immediately upon waking, Joseph did exactly as the angel had instructed him. God had spoken clearly; there was no reason to hesitate. This obedience came with the realization that there would be those who would misunderstand the situation and accuse one or both of them of immorality.

Three specific actions by Joseph are recorded in these verses. First, he took Mary as his wife with no further delay. There was never again a thought as to whether he should end the relationship. God had spoken; Joseph would act accordingly and immediately.

The second thing Joseph did was let Mary remain a virgin until after the birth of Jesus. The word "know" in Scripture is in certain contexts a euphemism for sexual activity. Matthew informed his readers that the virginity of Mary was indeed a fact. She conceived while a virgin and gave birth while still a virgin. The virgin birth of Christ is of utmost importance to us because it assures us of His divine nature and ability to be our Saviour.

The third thing Joseph did was name his son Jesus, as both he and Mary had been instructed (cf. Luke 1:31). The name "Jesus" was a common one among Jewish people, but for this particular son it had a special meaning. The Old Testament name "Joshua" (or "Hosea") is equivalent to "Jesus," also meaning "Yahweh is salvation."

—*Keith E. Eggert.*

QUESTIONS

1. What were the three phases of Jewish marriages, and how far apart were they?

2. What made Mary's pregnancy so shocking to Joseph?

3. What did Joseph do that demonstrated spiritual maturity?

4. What was Joseph planning to do, and how did God change his mind?

5. How does the Bible let us know that Joseph was not Jesus' physical father?

6. Why is the virgin birth of Jesus Christ so important?

7. Why did Matthew quote the Old Testament so much, and whom did he quote in Matthew 1?

8. What important truths should we glean from both Jesus' humanity and His deity?

9. What did Joseph do upon waking, and what was the risk to him?

10. What else did Joseph do following his dream?

—*Keith E. Eggert.*

PRACTICAL POINTS

1. From creating the universe to being the agent in the conception of the Saviour, the Spirit is sufficient to any need (Matt. 1:18; cf. Gen. 1:1-2).
2. The truly righteous loathe judging, for their righteousness is founded in love (Matt. 1:19).
3. God always supplies sufficient wisdom to those He calls to His service (vs. 20).
4. God brings about His most mighty works through people the world ignores (vs. 21).
5. Prophecy is the driving force behind the purposes of God in the world (vss. 22-23).
6. Once enlightened by God, the true servant is eager and careful to obey (vss. 24-25).

—John M. Lody.

RESEARCH AND DISCUSSION

1. Jesus has commanded us not to judge others; yet today it often seems that many Christians are eager to be first in line to judge the sins of others around them. Discuss this irony. What is the solution?
2. Discuss greatness in God's service. How do Christians evaluate a person's worth? Do we use God's standards, or are we influenced by the values of the world? Do we need change here?
3. God has made great promises to us through His prophets; but do we understand them as God intended, or are we confused? Discuss the importance of prophecy to our lives today.

—John M. Lody.

Golden Text Illuminated

"She shall bring forth a son, and thou shalt call his name JESUS: for he shall save his people from their sins" (Matthew 1:21).

After the angel told Joseph not to fear to take Mary as his wife, he assured him that she would bring forth a son. He also gave Joseph the responsibility of naming the child "Jesus."

The word "Jesus" is the Greek equivalent of the Hebrew word "Joshua," which means "Yahweh saves." This was a very appropriate name, because by Jesus alone, God would save sinners.

There are several senses in which Jesus came to save sinners. First, He came to save people from physical danger.

Second, He came to save people from the consequences of sin—both physical and eternal.

Third, He came to save people from the enslaving power of sin.

Fourth, He came to save people from the very presence of sin.

In Matthew 1:21, the sense being emphasized involves the temporal and eternal consequences of sin.

The heart of the mission of Christ was to save sinners from the terrible consequences of their sins.

In Matthew 1:21, the focus is on Jesus saving His people from their sins. This certainly refers to the Jews, but it does not exclude the Gentiles. The text does not say that He will save only Jews from their sins. The scope of His atonement is broadened in other passages to include all people. As John the Baptist said, "Behold the Lamb of God, which taketh away the sin of the world" (John 1:29).

—Karl Kloppmann.

Scripture Lesson Text

MATT. 2:7 Then Her'od, when he had privily called the wise men, enquired of them diligently what time the star appeared.

8 And he sent them to Beth'lehem, and said, Go and search diligently for the young child; and when ye have found *him,* **bring me word again, that I may come and worship him also.**

9 When they had heard the king, they departed; and, lo, the star, which they saw in the east, went before them, till it came and stood over where the young child was.

10 When they saw the star, they rejoiced with exceeding great joy.

16 Then Her'od, when he saw that he was mocked of the wise men, was exceeding wroth, and sent forth, and slew all the children that were in Beth'le-hem, and in all the coasts thereof, from two years old and under, according to the time which he had diligently enquired of the wise men.

17 Then was fulfilled that which was spoken by Jer'e-my the prophet, saying,

18 In Ra'ma was there a voice heard, lamentation, and weeping, and great mourning, Ra'chel weeping *for* her children, and would not be comforted, because they are not.

19 But when Her'od was dead, behold, an angel of the Lord appeareth in a dream to Jo'seph in E'gypt,

20 Saying, Arise, and take the young child and his mother, and go into the land of Is'ra-el: for they are dead which sought the young child's life.

21 And he arose, and took the young child and his mother, and came into the land of Is'ra-el.

22 But when he heard that Arche-la'us did reign in Ju-dae'a in the room of his father Her'od, he was afraid to go thither: notwithstanding, being warned of God in a dream, he turned aside into the parts of Gal'i-lee:

23 And he came and dwelt in a city called Naz'a-reth: that it might be fulfilled which was spoken by the prophets, He shall be called a Naz'a-rene.

Confirming Messiah's Birth

Lesson: Matthew 2:7-10, 16-23

Read: Matthew 2:1-23

TIME: 5 or 4 B.C.   PLACES: Jerusalem; Bethlehem; Egypt; Nazareth

---

GOLDEN TEXT—"When they saw the star, they rejoiced with exceeding great joy" (Matthew 2:10).

Lesson Exposition

Warren Wiersbe once wrote, "What a paradox that a babe in a manger should be called mighty! Yet even as a baby, Jesus Christ revealed power. His birth affected the heavens as that star appeared. The star affected the Magi, and they left their homes and made that long journey to Jerusalem. Their announcement shook King Herod and his court" ("His Name Is Wonderful," *Christianity Today,* vol. 30, no. 18). It is the amazing effect Jesus' birth had on the Magi and the shocking effect it had on Herod that we look at this week.

A SEARCH—Matt. 2:7-10

Herod's instruction (Matt. 2:7-8). "At first blush it would seem that he (Matthew) was getting out of the proper sphere of his argument by introducing the visit of the Eastern priest-sages, from the Gentile world. Further examination reveals, however, that one of the strongest proofs of His Messiahship was the homage of the Gentiles and the universal expectation which prevailed, not only in Palestine, but on the outside at the time of His birth" (Shepard, *The Christ of the Gospels,* Eerdmans).

The king was Herod the Great, who ruled in Judea from 37 to 4 B.C. (which is why the birth of Jesus is most often put near the year 4 B.C.). The Bible does not specify where the Magi were from, and they probably were not kings but men of a priestly caste who specialized in astronomy. Tradition says that they were from Parthia, which was near Babylon, nearly a thousand miles from Jerusalem.

When they arrived in Jerusalem and began asking where they could find this king of the Jews who had been born, Herod and many others became very troubled (Matt. 2:3). Herod first inquired of the priests and scribes concerning where this One was to be born. They answered by referring to Micah 5:2, where Bethlehem is specified as the birthplace of the coming Ruler of Israel. After receiving this information, Herod asked the Magi when the star they had referred to had first appeared.

From this question, from the fact that he inquired "diligently" (Matt. 2:7), and from his actions later, we can see that Herod was already devising a plan for getting rid of this rival. He posed his question in a secret meeting with the men lest his curiosity become known to those who were with Jesus. His instruction was just as devious, for we know for certain that he had no intention of worshiping the One he considered a threat to his throne.

The wise men's excitement (Matt. 2:9-10). It must have been shocking to the wise men to encounter a far-reaching lack of knowledge about the birth of the Messiah among His own people. God had planned for their confirmation of the event, however; so He made sure they did not give in to their discouragement. The information with which they left Jerusalem was incomplete, but it gave them incentive.

Imagine their pleasure upon the sudden reappearance of the star they had followed on such a long journey. They recognized that this was exactly the same star they had seen in their homelands, and this no doubt was the source of their joy. Apparently the star appeared as they were leaving Jerusalem and proceeded to take them to Bethlehem.

Not only that, but Matthew 2:9 tells us that it took them right to where Jesus was at the time. It "stood over where the young child was" and immediately stopped its movement.

A SLAUGHTER—Matt. 2:16-18

Herod's anger (Matt. 2:16). After the wise men saw Jesus, worshiped Him, and presented their gifts, they began their journey home. They did not honor Herod's request to let him know where they found the Child; God warned them in a dream not to do so (vs. 12).

The warning meant the wise men dared not return by going through Jerusalem. Once again they followed divine leading, and we are led to speculate that the men might have developed a real relationship with the God of Israel.

At the same time, God warned Joseph in a dream to immediately take Jesus to Egypt because Herod would try to find and kill Him (Matt. 2:13). So urgent was the need that Joseph left under cover of darkness. As soon as Herod realized the wise men were not returning to report to him, he became "exceeding wroth" (vs. 16), or enraged, about being "mocked." He immediately ordered the deaths of all male children under two years of age in Bethlehem and surrounding areas.

Putting together the fact that the wise men found Jesus in a house (Matt. 2:11) and Herod's use of the age of two for his decision leads us to realize that Jesus was not a baby in the manger when the wise men arrived. He was, instead, a little boy who was over a year old.

Jeremiah's fulfillment (Matt. 2:17-18). Herod was so evil that his anger caused him to act without reason or self-control. History has documented his evil character, and this was especially brought out against those he considered rivals to his throne. To order the killing of innocent children did not bother his conscience in the least. Because his heart was so hard, any reports he might have heard about weeping parents would not have affected him.

Jeremiah's statement quoted in Matthew 2:12-18 referred to the weeping of the nation at the time of the Babylonian Captivity. At that time, Ramah served as a staging point for the enemy (Jer. 40:1). Jeremiah himself had been taken there as a captive but was then released and allowed to return to Jerusalem. Rachel's tomb was near Bethlehem (Gen. 35:19), and she was mentioned here as the symbolic mother of the nation. The crying of the mothers in Bethlehem when Herod killed the babies was the same as that heard centuries earlier.

A SETTLING—Matt. 2:19-23

The angel's instruction (Matt. 2:19-21). Once again the angel of the Lord appeared to Joseph in a dream, this time telling him he could safely return to his homeland. When the angel told him in the previous dream that he should take Jesus and flee to Egypt, he also told him to stay there "until I bring thee word" (vs. 13); so he was now fulfilling that reassurance.

It would not have been safe for Joseph to take Jesus back to Israel as long as Herod was alive, because he would always consider Him to be a threat. So it was after Herod's death that the angel came with his message. Reference to those who sought Jesus' life probably means Herod primarily and others who were sympathetic with him and did his bidding. God's plan was being fulfilled.

As before, Joseph obeyed immediately, taking the young child and Mary back to Israel. We are not told in Scripture how long they had been in Egypt. We do know that God had made financial provision for them in advance of this journey. Joseph and Mary would probably have been unable to undertake such an unexpected trip without financial strain, but the gifts from the wise men would have covered their expenses.

Joseph's change of mind (Matt. 2:22-23). Herod's sons were no better than he was, and in fact, history documents plenty of evil in them also. When Joseph heard that Herod's son Archelaus was ruling in Judea, he felt endangered and afraid to return to Bethlehem. God confirmed his fears by appearing to him in a dream and warning him of the danger.

As a result, Joseph went farther north and settled in Galilee in the town of Nazareth. The ruler there was Antipas, who was also one of the sons of Herod but who was not such an evil and cruel ruler as were his father and brothers. Nazareth was a Roman military post and had a negative reputation (cf. John 1:46).

Once again Matthew quotes prophecy, this time in regard to making their home in Nazareth: "And he came and dwelt in a city called Nazareth: that it might be fulfilled which was spoken by the prophets, He shall be called a Nazarene" (2:23).

The Galileans were despised by the orthodox Jews of Judea; so maybe Matthew connected that idea with Isaiah 53:3, which says, "He is despised and rejected of men." However he was viewing the statement, we understand his intention of showing the Jews once again that Jesus was their Messiah.

—Keith E. Eggert.

QUESTIONS

1. Who called a private meeting with the Magi? Why?

2. How do we know that Herod began planning Jesus' death as soon as he heard about Him?

3. How specific was the leading of the star, and how did the wise men respond to seeing it again?

4. How did the Magi respond to Herod's desire to know the whereabouts of Jesus after they had visited Him?

5. How did God communicate to Joseph that he should flee to Egypt, and how did he respond?

6. How did Herod decide on the age of the babies he would order killed?

7. How did Matthew apply the quotation he used from Jeremiah?

8. When did it become safe for Joseph and Mary to return to Israel, and how did Joseph find out about this?

9. Why did Joseph make his home in Nazareth?

10. What is the source of Matthew's quotation about Jesus being called a Nazarene?

—Keith E. Eggert.

PRACTICAL POINTS

1. Evil always values secrecy, but the righteous have nothing to hide (Matt. 2:7).
2. Evil men are often adept at feigning piety to deceive the innocent (vs. 8).
3. The God of all the universe has infinite means at His disposal to ensure His purposes (vs. 9).
4. The hearts of God's people are filled with unspeakable joy at the sight of His works (vs. 10).
5. An evil man sees godly people as mocking and threatening, but God is his real enemy (vs. 16).
6. The ferocity of evil people, no matter how great, can never do any more than fulfill God's purposes (vss. 17-23).

—John M. Lody.

RESEARCH AND DISCUSSION

1. God's people have a right to privacy; but can it become merely an excuse to withhold the truth? How might we avoid using privacy to hide the truth?
2. From Cain to Judas, the Bible tells of false piety. How should God's people deal with the falsely religious? Find scriptural principles to guide you.
3. Jesus warned us of the world's hatred for His disciples (John 15:18); but why are people so ready to hate Jesus' disciples? What should our response be?
4. Discuss instances in which people's evil actions only served to fulfill God's purposes.

—John M. Lody.

Golden Text Illuminated

"When they saw the star, they rejoiced with exceeding great joy" (Matthew 2:10).

God often confirms His activities by simultaneously working in people's lives.

For example, an angel revealed to Mary that she would miraculously conceive the Son of God (Luke 1:32). After it was learned that she was pregnant, an angel also appeared to Joseph and gave him assurance that the Child was of the Holy Spirit (Matt. 1:20).

We again see the Lord working in a dual way in the birth of Christ. On the eve of His birth, God again confirmed His leading in Joseph and Mary's lives. He announced the Baby's birth to the shepherds.

The sudden, unexpected arrival of the wise men from the East is another example of God working in a dual way. These men from the East had supernaturally learned of the birth of Israel's Messiah.

In their home country, they saw an unusual star in the sky. They identified it as the star of Israel's Messiah. The identity of this star was most likely revealed to them in a supernatural manner.

It seems that this star disappeared until after they arrived in Bethlehem, where it once again appeared and led them directly to the house where the Christ Child was.

God was working not only in the lives of Joseph and Mary but also in the lives of the wise men from the East.

We can also see an example of God's dual working in Acts 15. When the church met to discuss a serious doctrinal issue, the apostles, elders, and brethren simultaneously felt the Lord's leading in their decision.

—Karl Kloppmann.

Scripture Lesson Text

MATT. 3:1 In those days came John the Bap'tist, preaching in the wilderness of Ju-dae'a,

2 And saying, Repent ye: for the kingdom of heaven is at hand.

3 For this is he that was spoken of by the prophet E-sa'ias, saying, The voice of one crying in the wilderness, Prepare ye the way of the Lord, make his paths straight.

4 And the same John had his raiment of camel's hair, and a leathern girdle about his loins; and his meat was locusts and wild honey.

5 Then went out to him Je-ru'sa-lem, and all Ju-dae'a, and all the region round about Jor'dan,

6 And were baptized of him in Jor'dan, confessing their sins.

11 I indeed baptize you with water unto repentance: but he that cometh after me is mightier than I, whose shoes I am not worthy to bear: he shall baptize you with the Ho'ly Ghost, and *with* fire:

12 Whose fan *is* in his hand, and he will throughly purge his floor, and gather his wheat into the garner; but he will burn up the chaff with unquenchable fire.

13 Then cometh Je'sus from Gal'i-lee to Jor'dan unto John, to be baptized of him.

14 But John forbad him, saying, I have need to be baptized of thee, and comest thou to me?

15 And Je'sus answering said unto him, Suffer *it to be so* now: for thus it becometh us to fulfil all righteousness. Then he suffered him.

16 And Je'sus, when he was baptized, went up straightway out of the water: and, lo, the heavens were opened unto him, and he saw the Spir'it of God descending like a dove, and lighting upon him:

17 And lo a voice from heaven, saying, This is my beloved Son, in whom I am well pleased.

Proclaimed in Baptism

Lesson: Matthew 3:1-6, 11-17

Read: Matthew 3:1-17

TIME: A.D. 26   PLACE: wilderness of Judea

GOLDEN TEXT—"Lo a voice from heaven, saying, This is my beloved Son, in whom I am well pleased" (Matthew 3:17).

Lesson Exposition

Baptism is a matter of obedience to the Lord's command, but it is also our testimony to others of our salvation. We remember that the Ethiopian eunuch immediately wanted to be baptized after Philip taught him about salvation through Jesus Christ (Acts 8:36-38).

This week it is the baptism of Jesus Himself that we examine. There are many who wonder why Jesus would want to be baptized, for it certainly was not an act that followed salvation for Him. We will see what He told John.

THE MINISTRY OF JOHN— Matt. 3:1-6

Preaching of repentance (Matt. 3:1-2). Matthew, in his record of the life of Jesus, jumped ahead nearly thirty years after telling of His birth and sojourn in Egypt. We know almost nothing about the boyhood of Jesus except for Luke's account of His trip to Jerusalem when He was twelve years of age (Luke 2:41-51).

John was the son of a priest and had the privilege and right to follow in his father's footsteps. But Matthew says he went out to the wilderness of Judea to preach instead of ministering in the temple in Jerusalem. That in itself must have said to the people that this man was unique and had a significant message. It was an urgent message, and he sounded much like some of the prophets of old. After all, the Messiah was present on earth and about to make His appearance!

Here was the forerunner of the Messiah, the ambassador of the King. His message revolved around the word "repent," the same word Jesus would later use.

"His message . . . had two parts: (1) a soteriological aspect, repent, and (2) an eschatological aspect, for the kingdom of heaven is near. The concept of a coming kingdom was well known in Old Testament Scriptures. But the idea that repentance was necessary in order to enter this kingdom was something new and became a stumbling block to many Jews. They thought that as children of Abraham they would automatically be granted entrance into Messiah's kingdom" (Walvoord and Zuck, eds., *The Bible Knowledge Commentary,* Victor).

To repent means to have a change of mind with an accompanying change of direction in life. It is a turning around that results in a different manner of living. The Jews, especially their religious leaders, would have problems with such a message, since acceptance into God's kingdom was supposedly automatic for them. The possibility of their not getting there was offensive to them.

Fulfilling of prophecy (Matt. 3:3-4). Matthew wrote that John the Baptist was the fulfillment of one of Isaiah's prophecies (Isa. 40:3). So significant was the appearance and ministry of this man that all four Gospel writers mentioned him and quoted this verse (cf. Mark 1:3; Luke 3:4-5; John 1:23).

Isaiah 40 is a turning point in the prophet's written message. In the first thirty-nine chapters, he pronounced judgment on many nations, but chapter 40 begins with a message of comfort and salvation for Israel. In Isaiah's day the message would be first and foremost for Judah, whose sins would end up being severely judged by God. The Jews of John's day should have been able to connect that message of restoration with the Messiah's coming in order to restore them to God by the establishment of His promised kingdom. John was pointing to the coming King.

John's clothing and food clearly separated him from the current religious system and its leaders. He was dressed like Elijah (II Kings 1:8) and preached a straightforward message like Elijah. His food was that of common poor people instead of the luxurious foods of the religious leadership. His entire manner of living appealed to the people who were earnestly listening for a message from God.

Baptizing of converts (Matt. 3:5-6). People kept flowing out to hear this preacher by the Jordan River. They came not only from the city of Jerusalem but also from the entire province of Judea and all over the Jordan Valley. The excitement engendered by this man, the first in over four hundred years to speak prophetically, was unprecedented.

Matthew 3:7 indicates the Pharisees and Sadducees were there too. When John saw them, he railed against them for their hypocrisy, warning them that they too should repent and prove their repentance by their lives (vs. 8). They were in danger of facing judgment (vss. 9-10). The common people coming with sincere hearts, however, confessed their sins and were baptized as a testimony of their change of heart.

John's baptism was different from Christian baptism. Those being baptized were doing so in anticipation of the arrival of the Messiah. When we are baptized, we are identifying ourselves with Christ in His death, burial, and resurrection.

THE PREPARATION OF JESUS— Matt. 3:11-17

Jesus' superiority (Matt. 3:11-12). When people voluntarily entered the water of the Jordan River to be baptized, they were demonstrating their repentance.

While this was good, something better was coming. The Person coming next was far superior to John, and His ministry would be much more effective than his. This One was so far superior to him that he, John, was not worthy to carry His sandals (undo and remove them, which was the most menial task of the lowest servant). The One coming would baptize not with water but with the Holy Spirit and fire.

From the context there seems to be merit to viewing this as a single event. Matthew 3:12 refers to the refining process that will occur under the Messiah. Just as a winnowing fork tossed grain in the air and led to the separation of the grain and chaff, so the Messiah will separate believers and unbelievers. Believers will enter the kingdom, while unbelievers will be taken away for destruction (cf. 24:36-44).

Jesus' baptism (Matt. 3:13-15). When Jesus Himself appeared in order to be baptized, John tried to prevent

Him from doing so. John would naturally have assumed that since his baptism was evidence of repentance and Jesus had no need for repentance, there was no reason for Him to be baptized. Since he recognized himself as being far inferior to Jesus, John stated that he was the one who needed to be baptized by Jesus rather than the other way around. However, Jesus insisted they go ahead with the ritual.

Jesus said He should be baptized, "for thus it becometh us to fulfil all righteousness" (Matt. 3:15). What did He mean by this? Jesus came to provide righteousness for sinners. In order to be identified with the sinners He came to save, He needed to be baptized just as they were. He was also identifying Himself with those who had already been baptized by John. Jesus' baptism, therefore, seems to have been primarily for the purpose of becoming identified with those He came to save. In this He was accomplishing His Father's will.

Jesus' affirmation (Matt. 3:16-17). As soon as Jesus came up out of the water, He immediately received affirmation from both of the other Members of the Godhead. First, heaven opened; Jesus (and John) then saw the Holy Spirit descending in the bodily form of a dove and alighting upon Him (John 1:32). This was the moment of His anointing into public ministry. The form of a bird is not the most important factor; the gentle, active presence of the Spirit revealed to the people who He was and why He had come.

The second act of affirmation came from the Father when a voice suddenly spoke from heaven, saying, "This is my beloved Son, in whom I am well pleased" (Matt. 3:17). Both Mark (1:11) and Luke (3:22) record this as a personal statement to Jesus by saying the voice said "Thou art" instead of "This is." As with the Spirit's descent, we cannot know for certain whether the people saw and heard what happened; but the use of "this is" seems to indicate that God spoke to the crowd too.

"The phrase 'in whom I am well pleased' means that the Father takes great delight, pleasure, and satisfaction in the Son. The verb in Greek conveys that God's pleasure in the Son is constant. He has always taken pleasure in His Son" (Osborne and Comfort, eds., *Life Application Bible Commentary,* Tyndale). The time had finally come for God's Son to begin His earthly ministry.

—Keith E. Eggert.

QUESTIONS

1. What was so unusual about John carrying out his ministry in the wilderness?

2. What were the two parts of the message John presented?

3. What does "repent" mean, and why were some Jews offended by being told that they needed to repent?

4. What was John doing according to the quotation from Isaiah 40:3?

5. Whom did John criticize at his baptisms?

6. How was John's baptism different from Christian baptism, and how was Jesus' different from both?

7. In what way did John say Jesus' coming ministry would be superior to his, and what might this have meant?

8. Why did John not want to baptize Jesus, and what was Jesus' answer?

9. What might Jesus have meant when He insisted that He be baptized?

10. By whom was Jesus affirmed immediately after His baptism, and what happened at that time?

—Keith E. Eggert.

PRACTICAL POINTS

1. If God's people have lapsed into complacency, He will confront them in a way that will shock them out of it (Matt. 3:1-4).

2. When God confronts our sin, many will be repelled, but God's Spirit will gather whom He chooses (vss. 5-6).

3. Confronting sin is essential, but saving is always a mightier work than judging (vss. 11-12).

4. God's way is always one of humility and submission to authority (vss. 13-15).

5. God's calling is never alone; He always supplies the needed power and motivation for it (vs. 16).

6. God's pleasure is in Jesus and whoever belongs to Him (vs. 17).

—John M. Lody.

RESEARCH AND DISCUSSION

1. Have God's people become too comfortable and complacent today? Can you see God confronting our complacency in the world today? Are we responding to Him?

2. Discuss the varying reactions people exhibit when confronted with their sin. What factors make the difference between those who repent and those who merely justify themselves?

3. Discuss Jesus as our model for humility. Who has more reason to be humble, you or Him? Why is pride such a problem for people?

4. Discuss God's calling of a person to special ministry. What characteristics seem to mark a true calling from God?

—John M. Lody.

Golden Text Illuminated

"Lo a voice from heaven, saying, This is my beloved Son, in whom I am well pleased" (Matthew 3:17).

When Jesus was baptized by John in the Jordan, many significant things happened.

First, in the rite of water baptism, Jesus identified Himself with sinners. John's baptism was a rite that people submitted to in order to express repentance of their sin (Matt. 3:6, 11).

Jesus had no sin (I John 3:5), so His baptism could not have symbolized repentance from sin. Then why was He baptized? One reason was "to fulfil all righteousness" (Matt. 3:15). It was a righteous thing to do.

Another reason was to display His humble heart. It was a great act of humility for the superior to be baptized by the inferior. John immediately saw that it was out of order for him to baptize Jesus. He tried to stop Him and said, "I have need to be baptized of thee" (Matt. 3:14).

A second thing that happened when Jesus was baptized was the coming of the Holy Spirit upon Him, anointing Him for His ministry (Matt. 3:16; Acts 10:38).

The Holy Spirit descended from heaven in the form of a dove and landed on Jesus. This confirmed to John that Jesus was the promised Messiah (John 1:33).

A third thing that happened when Jesus was baptized was that God spoke audible words from heaven, confirming that Jesus was His dear Son.

Besides these three significant things, something else contributed to the magnitude of Jesus' baptism. At the baptism of Jesus we get a glimpse of the holy Trinity.

—Karl Kloppmann.

Scripture Lesson Text

MATT. 4:1 Then was Je'sus led up of the Spir'it into the wilderness to be tempted of the devil.

2 And when he had fasted forty days and forty nights, he was afterward an hungred.

3 And when the tempter came to him, he said, If thou be the Son of God, command that these stones be made bread.

4 But he answered and said, It is written, Man shall not live by bread alone, but by every word that proceedeth out of the mouth of God.

5 Then the devil taketh him up into the holy city, and setteth him on a pinnacle of the temple,

6 And saith unto him, If thou be the Son of God, cast thyself down: for it is written, He shall give his angels charge concerning thee:

and in *their* hands they shall bear thee up, lest at any time thou dash thy foot against a stone.

7 Je'sus said unto him, It is written again, Thou shalt not tempt the Lord thy God.

8 Again, the devil taketh him up into an exceeding high mountain, and sheweth him all the kingdoms of the world, and the glory of them;

9 And saith unto him, All these things will I give thee, if thou wilt fall down and worship me.

10 Then saith Je'sus unto him, Get thee hence, Sa'tan: for it is written, Thou shalt worship the Lord thy God, and him only shalt thou serve.

11 Then the devil leaveth him, and, behold, angels came and ministered unto him.

Strengthened in Temptation

Lesson: Matthew 4:1-11

Read: Matthew 4:1-11

TIME: A.D. 26   PLACE: wilderness of Judea

GOLDEN TEXT—"Then saith Jesus unto him, Get thee hence, Satan: for it is written, Thou shalt worship the Lord thy God, and him only shalt thou serve" (Matthew 4:10).

Lesson Exposition

SATISFY YOURSELF—Matt. 4:1-4

Jesus' hunger (Matt. 4:1-2). Is it not an amazing fact that the same Holy Spirit who anointed Jesus for ministry at His baptism then led Him purposely into a wilderness setting to be tempted by the devil? It happened immediately after His baptism, as determined by the word "then" beginning this chapter. Since Jesus was led so purposely, it was actually God who took the offensive in this experience. With such definite direction, it appears that it would not have been possible for Satan to escape this humiliating situation.

We should also realize from this passage that the devil is real. The Greek word for "devil" means "accuser," and he is not simply a symbolic figment of someone's imagination. He is a fallen angel determined to destroy as much of God's plan for mankind as he possibly can.

Satan's temptation (Matt. 4:3). When Jesus was at a very vulnerable stage of hunger, having had nothing to eat for forty days, Satan started his temptation by appealing to that vulnerability. He does not usually tempt any of us in our area of real strength;

rather, he repeatedly tempts us where he knows we are weak and vulnerable. The fact that Jesus was the Son of God did not exempt Him from experiencing the natural hunger resulting from going without food for a long period of time.

When Satan said, "If thou be the Son of God" (Matt. 4:3), he was not expressing doubt about the fact. He was fully aware of who Jesus was. What he actually meant was "Since You truly are the Son of God, You have the power to do something about Your hunger. In fact, You have the power to turn the stones around You into bread." This was true, of course. Satan was not trying to get Jesus to doubt that He was the Son of God. Rather, he was telling Him to act independently of His Father. He should go ahead and satisfy Himself by His power.

At that time, however, it was the Father's will for Jesus to be hungry even while surrounded by stones He could turn into bread. He dared not do what Satan suggested.

Jesus' response (Matt. 4:4). Jesus had no problem with miraculously providing food when it was needed. When five thousand men (plus women and children) had been listening to Him teach all day long and evening arrived without food, Jesus took five loaves of bread and two fish and multiplied them to feed everyone (14:13-21). Later, when a multitude of people had been following Him for three days without food, He again fed them by multiplying seven loaves of bread and a few fish (15:32-38).

But Jesus could be hungry and still be satisfied, knowing He was doing His Father's will. We too can be deprived but content when we are certain we are living in His will.

PROVE YOURSELF—Matt. 4:5-7

Satan's lure (Matt. 4:5-6). Satan next took Jesus to the highest pinnacle of the temple, which would have been the southeast corner of the temple complex overlooking the Kidron Valley. It was a setting in which Jesus could dramatically prove Himself by a spectacular display. Imagine the oohs and ahs coming from anyone watching Him leap off and then land without harm. That would certainly be something no one had ever done before, and it would surely prove that Jesus was more than a mere human being.

For Jesus to throw Himself off the temple in a display that would awe and satisfy people would not be God's way of revealing Himself. He would prove Himself in other ways through regular daily ministries but not in spectacular displays. People would come to believe in Him as He ministered in ways that fulfilled Scripture (Matt. 11:4-6).

It should be a warning to us that Satan knows Scripture and how to use it for his own benefit. There are times when well-meaning people might lead us astray by giving bad advice based on some Bible verse. False doctrines are built upon selective truths found in the Bible. We must stay aware and follow Christ's teachings carefully.

Jesus' reply (Matt. 4:7). Jesus' answer was another quote from Deuteronomy, specifically, 6:16: "Ye shall not tempt the Lord your God, as ye tempted him in Massah." God had Moses strike a rock with his rod and provide water from the rock (Exod. 17:6). He then called the place "Massah, and Meribah" (vs. 7). Moses explained his naming of the place this way: "And he called the name of the place Massah, and Meribah, because of the chiding of the children of Israel, and because they tempted the Lord, saying, Is the Lord among us, or not?"

This is the tempting referred to in Deuteronomy 6:16, which in turn is what Jesus quoted to Satan at this second temptation. The Greek word translated "tempt" means "to test thoroughly." Jesus could have jumped, knowing His Father would protect Him. Angels could have landed Him safely. However, for Jesus to leap off the high point of the temple as Satan suggested would be nothing more than a test of the Father. It is wrong to put God in this kind of situation.

PROFIT YOURSELF—Matt. 4:8-11

Satan's offer (Matt. 4:8-9). It is God's plan for His Son to one day rule the world (cf. Ps. 2). Satan's final test related to that plan, for it gave Jesus the opportunity to secure that position immediately instead of having to go by way of the cross. While God's plan was for a restored kingdom after the suffering and death of His Son, Satan offered something seemingly better: Jesus could have that kingdom and all the glory associated with it without having to suffer. It was really such a simple plan.

From "an exceeding high mountain" (Matt. 4:8), Satan showed Jesus all the kingdoms of the world at once (Luke 4:5 says it was in "a moment of time"). What this magnificent scene was really like is beyond our comprehension, and how this happened is not explained in detail. What we do know is that Satan's offer was legitimate, for he is "the prince of the power of the air" (Eph. 2:2) and "the god of this world" (II Cor. 4:4).

We understand that Satan's control is limited to what God allows, but right now God is allowing him a great deal of authority in the world. Until that time when Jesus is the undisputed ruler of this world, Satan will continue to exercise enormous amounts of influence on human beings.

This gives us an insight into how the devil will often tempt us. He said in essence that he could give Jesus something in a better way than God could. If He would take a different direction, He could more easily have what He desired. How often have we veered slightly away from God's Word and will in hopes of achieving something in an easier way! We then found out the hard way that it is always best to do things God's way, no matter the cost.

Jesus' command (Matt. 4:10-11). God's law demanded both worship and service from His people. Whenever a person truly worships, he does so from a willingness to serve and please. If one pays homage to a superior, he expresses at the same time a desire to do his wishes. The close relationship of these two is seen in Jesus' command to Satan. He first gave an authoritative command for Satan to leave. Then He quoted from Deuteronomy 6:13 and 10:20 to show that Scripture clearly prohibits the worship of anyone but God.

What Jesus quoted mentions both worship and service, implying that the two go together. Satan conveniently did not ask for service, just worship, but Jesus knew what he was seeking. "Satan's departure from Jesus followed the King's authoritative command, 'Away from Me, Satan!' It is ironic that Satan had just offered to be the benevolent master to Jesus, but Jesus' authoritative response and Satan's cowering obedience demonstrated who was the real Master" (Anders and Weber, *Holman New Testament Commentary,* Broadman & Holman).

Was Jesus tempted only here in the wilderness and only these three times? Luke 4:13 indicates otherwise. We know He "was in all points tempted like as we are" (Heb. 4:15); so He may have been tempted many other times. What is encouraging is to know that just as Jesus defeated Satan through the use of God's Word, so we can too. He has proved Himself to be our example.

—Keith E. Eggert.

QUESTIONS

1. How did it happen that after His baptism, Jesus ended up in the wilderness to be tempted by Satan?

2. What should we learn about Satan from this incident?

3. What was the setting for Jesus' first temptation, and what did Satan suggest He do about it?

4. What does Jesus' answer to this temptation mean to us?

5. What was Satan's second temptation, and what kind of warning does this give us?

6. Why would it have been wrong for Jesus to jump off the temple?

7. What was Satan's third temptation and offer?

8. What was the real temptation in offering Jesus something that He was already assured of having in the future?

9. How did Jesus end the temptation, and what does this teach today?

10. Was this Jesus' only time to be tempted?

—Keith E. Eggert.

PRACTICAL POINTS

1. If the perfect Son of God had to endure testing, how much more do we (Matt. 4:1)?
2. Testing comes to us in our direst need (vss. 2-3).
3. Even the satisfaction of a true need is not right if not done the right way (vss. 4-5).
4. The Lord's prerogative is to test us, but for us to test Him shows faithlessness (vss. 6-7).
5. All worldly powers pale in comparison with the power of one's faithfulness to God (vss. 8-10).
6. When the testing of our faith is complete, if we have endured it faithfully, God's comfort and encouragement will be upon us, never to forsake us (vs. 11).

—John M. Lody.

RESEARCH AND DISCUSSION

1. Discuss Jesus' temptations. Why did the perfect, divine, God-Man need to be tested? What does this say about our prospects of avoiding God's testing of our own faith?
2. Why would it have been wrong for Jesus to make stones into bread after fasting for so long? When does the meeting of a normal need become wrong?
3. Discuss whether it is ever right to put God to a test. Why or why not? Use Scripture to support your answer.
4. How does testing come to us? Does God test us, or is it Satan? Do we bring testing upon ourselves? Explain and support your answers from Scripture.

—John M. Lody.

Golden Text Illuminated

"Then saith Jesus unto him, Get thee hence, Satan: for it is written, Thou shalt worship the Lord thy God, and him only shalt thou serve" (Matthew 4:10).

We need to be alert for Satan's shortcuts and firmly resist them as the Lord did on this occasion. When faced with Satan's powerful temptation, Jesus stood His ground by quoting from a specific verse of Scripture (Deut. 6:13). The verse He quoted word for word declared that only God should be worshiped. Satan saw Jesus' firm reliance upon God's Word and left Him.

It is worth noting that Satan did not say "Bow down and worship me only." He only asked to become one of Jesus' objects of worship. Satan allows people to worship God as long as they worship him too. Satan knows that God will not receive worship unless it is exclusively focused on Him; anything else is idolatry.

In Old Testament times, Israel was often involved in worshiping God along with many false deities. Such pluralistic worship denies that God alone is the true and living God (I Tim. 1:17).

According to Matthew 4:10, serving is an expression of worship. Many believers do not worship Satan in a theological sense, but they do so in a practical sense. By doing the devil's will in certain areas of their lives, they serve him. It is a form of worship and thus idolatry.

When it comes to effectively resisting Satan's temptation, there is no better method than quoting specific, appropriate verses of Scripture. This was the Lord's method, and He is our example.

—Karl Kloppmann.

Scripture Lesson Text

MATT. 9:27 And when Je′sus departed thence, two blind men followed him, crying, and saying, *Thou* Son of Da′vid, have mercy on us.

28 And when he was come into the house, the blind men came to him: and Je′sus saith unto them, Believe ye that I am able to do this? They said unto him, Yea, Lord.

29 Then touched he their eyes, saying, According to your faith be it unto you.

30 And their eyes were opened; and Je′sus straitly charged them, saying, See *that* **no man know** *it.*

31 But they, when they were departed, spread abroad his fame in all that country.

32 As they went out, behold, they brought to him a dumb man possessed with a devil.

33 And when the devil was cast out, the dumb spake: and the multitudes marvelled, saying, It was never so seen in Is′ra-el.

34 But the Phar′i-sees said, He casteth out devils through the prince of the devils.

11:2 Now when John had heard in the prison the works of Christ, he sent two of his disciples,

3 And said unto him, Art thou he that should come, or do we look for another?

4 Je′sus answered and said unto them, Go and shew John again those things which ye do hear and see:

5 The blind receive their sight, and the lame walk, the lepers are cleansed, and the deaf hear, the dead are raised up, and the poor have the gospel preached to them.

6 And blessed is *he,* whosoever shall not be offended in me.

Demonstrated in Acts of Healing

Lesson: Matthew 9:27-34; 11:2-6

Read: Matthew 9:27-34; 11:2-6

TIME: A.D. 28   PLACE: Galilee

GOLDEN TEXT — "The blind receive their sight, and the lame walk, the lepers are cleansed, and the deaf hear, the dead are raised up, and the poor have the gospel preached to them" (Matthew 11:5).

Lesson Exposition

HEALING THE BLIND— Matt. 9:27-31

Two blind men (Matt. 9:27). Jesus had just been in the home of Jairus, one of the rulers of the synagogue, where He had restored Jairus's daughter to life (Matt. 9:18-26; cf. Mark 5:22). It was upon leaving that place that He encountered two blind men who followed Him while crying out for His help.

These blind men had insight into who this Person was, for they called out to Him as the Son of David. This apparently is the first time this messianic title was used, and it revealed that they were appealing for a miracle that only the Messiah was capable of performing. They had obviously heard things about Jesus' ministry and believed that He was the promised Messiah and could do what they desired. They were already well ahead of many people (especially the religious leaders) in their understanding.

What they requested was mercy, and their appeal was based on their knowledge that Jesus was the Son of David.

The Greek word used in Matthew 9:27 refers to having compassion or taking pity on someone. They had a need and knew who could have compassion on them.

Their healing (Matt. 9:28-29). Jesus did not stop on the road to respond to the calls of the men but continued instead to the house where He was going. Although the house is not identified, it was probably that of Peter, where He might have often stayed when He was in Capernaum (8:14). He apparently did not want to perform another miracle in the presence of the multitudes; so He waited until He was in the seclusion of a house to address the blind men. They were allowed to enter, even though not many others were.

"Believe ye that I am able to do this?" (Matt. 9:28). If they expected Jesus to do what only the Messiah could do, the blind men had to have faith in Him. Their response revealed that they did, and He immediately responded by touching and healing them. Jesus was never afraid to touch those who needed Him to minister to them, including those with leprosy (8:1-3). He never hesitates to "touch" us spiritually when we need Him, but we must notice His response: "According to your faith be it unto you" (9:29).

Their excitement (Matt. 9:30-31). As soon as Jesus spoke those words, the blindness left, giving evidence that the men did indeed possess faith. Jesus immediately instructed them sternly that they should not go around telling people what had happened.

Earlier Jesus had healed a leper and given him the same order (Matt. 8:4). Mark 1:40-45 also records that incident. When that man disobeyed Jesus by spreading the word about what He had done, it affected His ministry greatly. He had to relocate outside the city and away from the masses to have the opportunity to be heard properly.

These men also disobeyed, but we sense that it was because of their excitement over being healed. Jesus' stern warning was not enough to contain the wonder of their deliverance from a long-time handicap. Those of us who have experienced outstanding blessing from the Lord can relate to their enthusiasm. Sometimes things that happen are simply too exciting not to share with others.

HEALING THE DEMON POSSESSED—Matt. 9:32-34

Casting out a demon (Matt. 9:32-33). Once again, as Jesus left the building, He was met with someone in need. We cannot tell who "they" were who brought this man, but presumably they were relatives or good friends concerned about his welfare. Matthew appears to continue proving what was stated in Isaiah 35:5-6. This man was mute and demon possessed. It was not always the case that demons in a person caused an inability to speak, but in this man they had. His muteness was not from natural medical causes but was brought on by the demon.

Jesus cast the demon out of this man, who was immediately freed from his muteness.

Accusing Jesus of wrongdoing (Matt. 9:34). The Pharisees were not enamored. Instead, they had an evil explanation: "He casteth out devils through the prince of the devils." While the crowds were wondering whether Jesus might be the Messiah, the religious leaders rejected the implications that were clear in His miracles. Since they could not deny the reality of the miracle, they had to explain it in another way.

It is a fact of life that those in leadership positions often do not lead according to the truth. An Old Testament example is found in Jeremiah 36. When Jeremiah's scroll was read in the temple, Michaiah was listening and reported to the princes. They, in turn, asked to have it read to them. Their response was one of fear (vs. 16). When it was read to the king, however, he cut it up and burned it in the fire and in so doing removed the fear of his princes. Such leaders will answer to God one day and have great regret.

ANSWERING JOHN'S QUESTION— Matt. 11:2-6

John's confusion (Matt. 11:2-3). Chapter 10 records how Jesus called His disciples and instructed them about their ministry before sending them out. Matthew 11:1 says that He left on a teaching and preaching mission. Whether or not He sent the disciples out by themselves here is not clear, even though it is implied. They were very inexperienced and had much to learn.

John had previously preached that Messiah was coming to execute judgment, but he was not hearing anything about this in his prison cell. There are those who accuse John of losing faith, saying that the question sent by two of his disciples reveals that he was doubting. He did ask whether Jesus was the One. After his experience at Jesus' baptism, it seems unlikely that this man of great faith would come to the point of doubt, for that had been a time of confirmation. But it is understandable why he would have had questions.

It might be that John was getting concerned that Jesus was not fulfilling the words of condemnation he had previously preached. Was it more a matter of impatience than doubt? Perhaps John wondered whether he had misunderstood Messiah's agenda. Why was He not moving more aggressively and accomplishing the victories He was expected to have? Why was He being rejected by so many and doing nothing about it? Maybe John wondered why he, as Messiah's forerunner, was in prison. He needed clarification about what was happening.

Jesus' explanation (Matt. 11:4-6). According to Luke 7:21-22, Jesus was busy when John's disciples arrived. When Jesus answered these disciples, He simply pointed out that they should go back and tell John what they were witnessing at that very moment. He then referred to the very things prophesied in Isaiah about the Messiah's ministry (35:5-6). He made no other defense for Himself.

Jesus' words were the assurance and confirmation John needed. Being the godly man he was, John would have understood immediately what Jesus meant. He might also have recalled other words in Isaiah: "And in that day shall the deaf hear the words of the book, and the eyes of the blind shall see out of obscurity, and out of darkness. The meek also shall increase their joy in the Lord, and the poor among men shall rejoice in the Holy One of Israel" (29:18-19).

Jesus concluded by saying, "Blessed is he, whosoever shall not be offended in me" (Matt. 11:6). Since John wondered about His activities, others probably did too. They needed to exercise faith, not doubt, and should not be offended by His ministry.

"Those who did not miss the true character of the Lord would be truly blessed. Though He will ultimately bring judgment to this world by judging sin when He brings in His kingdom, the timing then was not appropriate. Israel's rejection of Him was causing a postponement in establishing the physical kingdom. But all, including John, who truly perceived the person and work of Christ would be blessed" (Walvoord and Zuck, eds., *The Bible Knowledge Commentary,* Victor).
—Keith E. Eggert.

QUESTIONS

1. Whom did Jesus meet as He left Jairus's home?

2. What did they call Jesus, and what did this indicate about their knowledge of Him?

3. Why did He delay His response to them until He was in a house?

4. What happened after He told them not to tell about their healing, and why did He tell them this?

5. What was the need of the man Jesus met later, and what caused the need?

6. What explanation did the religious leaders offer for what Jesus did for this man?

7. What circumstances led John to send two disciples to Jesus, and what was their question for Him?

8. What might have led John to ask this question of Jesus?

9. How did Jesus respond, and what prophet prophesied of His acts?

10. Why was it important for Jesus to say, "Blessed is he, whosoever shall not be offended in me" (Matt. 11:6)?
—Keith E. Eggert.

PRACTICAL POINTS

1. Need begets desire, desire begets hope, hope begets faith, and faith begets salvation (Matt. 9:27-30).
2. The joy of God's salvation cannot be restrained (vs. 31).
3. When God undeniably manifests His glory and goodness, His enemies will persist and call it evil (vss. 32-34).
4. When we are in great distress, even the most faithful will be tempted to doubt (11:2-3).
5. Tragedies can make us forget God's love, but remembering it restores our faith (vss. 4-5).
6. He who holds fast to his faith in God while others fall away is greatly blessed (vs. 6).

—John M. Lody.

RESEARCH AND DISCUSSION

1. Discuss the relationship between human need and salvation. (Review Luke 7:47; 16:19-31; 17:12-19; 18:10-14.) What should be our attitude toward those in great need?
2. Why did the blind men in Matthew 9:27-31 not keep silent as Jesus commanded? Did they sin? Why or why not? Discuss your answers.
3. Have there been times when tragedies have tempted you to doubt God? Share and discuss doubt as part of a Christian's life.
4. Have you ever felt ashamed or embarrassed about being a Christian? Share and discuss standing up for Christ amid hostility.

—John M. Lody.

Golden Text Illuminated

"The blind receive their sight, and the lame walk, the lepers are cleansed, and the deaf hear, the dead are raised up, and the poor have the gospel preached to them" (Matthew 11:5).

These miracles were irrefutable proof that Jesus was the promised One.

Although Jesus' miracles were often acts of mercy toward people who were suffering, the primary purpose of His miracles was to authenticate Him as the promised Messiah of the Old Testament. This can be seen in the way He pointed John the Baptist to His miracles as evidence that He was the Christ.

That the miracles of Jesus were primarily signs of who He was can also be seen in other biblical references. For example, when Peter preached on the Day of Pentecost, he spoke of Jesus as "a man approved of God among you by miracles and wonders and signs" (Acts 2:22). His miracles were God's captivating way of saying, "This is my beloved Son: hear him" (Mark 9:7).

The authenticating nature of His many miraculous deeds can also be observed in the purpose of the Gospel of John. The Apostle John wrote, "And many other signs truly did Jesus in the presence of his disciples, which are not written in this book: but these are written that ye might believe that Jesus is the Christ, the Son of God" (20:30-31).

Some say that Jesus must perform signs and wonders today so that people will believe in Him. The Apostle John indicates, however, that the recorded signs of Christ are sufficient to inspire belief today.

—Karl Kloppmann.

Scripture Lesson Text

MATT. 11:25 At that time Je′sus answered and said, I thank thee, O Father, Lord of heaven and earth, because thou hast hid these things from the wise and prudent, and hast revealed them unto babes.

26 Even so, Father: for so it seemed good in thy sight.

27 All things are delivered unto me of my Father: and no man knoweth the Son, but the Father; neither knoweth any man the Father, save the Son, and *he* to whomsoever the Son will reveal *him*.

28 Come unto me, all *ye* that labour and are heavy laden, and I will give you rest.

29 Take my yoke upon you, and learn of me; for I am meek and lowly in heart: and ye shall find rest unto your souls.

30 For my yoke *is* easy, and my burden is light.

Declared in Prayer

Lesson: Matthew 11:25-30

Read: Matthew 11:25-30

TIME: A.D. 28   PLACE: Galilee

GOLDEN TEXT—"Come unto me, all ye that labour and are heavy laden, and I will give you rest" (Matthew 11:28).

Lesson Exposition

JESUS REVEALED—Matt. 11:25-27

Hidden from some, revealed to others (Matt. 11:25-26). In these two verses, Jesus addressed His Father, to whom He referred as "Lord of heaven and earth." "Lord" refers to someone supreme in authority and thus in complete control. It is good for us to remember this about God, for when our lives take a turn we do not expect and do not like, we can still be certain that He is in control.

Jesus gave particular thanks for the fact that His Father has hidden certain things from the wise and prudent and revealed them instead to what Jesus called "babes" (Matt. 11:25). It is an interesting contrast, for we would not normally contrast wise and prudent people with babies. We would instead contrast those who are wise with those who are foolish. This must be a contrast of those who know things with those who do not.

In fact, Jesus' thought was a contrast of those who think they know things with those who realize they do not. He said that they needed to be like children. It is childlike faith that results in salvation and dependent daily living for the believer. His mention of the "wise and prudent" (Matt. 11: 25) was a sarcastic reference to those who relied on their own understanding of things and felt confident in themselves.

Those who are determined to live by their own standards instead of those of God will never be given revelation about spiritual things, in spite of the fact that they might be wise in worldly matters. This is the way God has determined things to be, and for this Jesus was expressing thanksgiving.

Knowing the Son, knowing the Father (Matt. 11:27). We must focus on the statement "All things are delivered unto me of my father." The entire administration of God's kingdom has been given to His Son. Matthew continued by quoting Jesus saying that knowing the Son completely is not possible for humans but for His Father alone. Nor is it possible to know the Father unless Jesus, the Son, chooses to reveal Him. Jesus' statement that He and the Father are mutually and exclusively known to each other is a clear indication of equality. Jesus is God just as much as the Father is God. He is fully God and fully man.

This was absolutely necessary if He was going to atone for mankind's sin.

Had He been only man, He could not have done that; had He been only God, He could not have died.

JESUS APPROACHABLE— Matt. 11:28-30

Invitation to come (Matt. 11:28). The Jews listening to Jesus that day were trying to live successfully and acceptably under the religious load imposed upon them by their religious leaders. Imagine the sense of relief upon hearing this invitation from Jesus! He was not haranguing them about adhering to a long list of regulations. Instead, He was simply inviting them to come to Him. He was there offering Himself as the One who could put them into a right relationship with God; all they had to do was accept.

In our culture, many are very tired of life the way they are living it and are longing for some kind of meaningful change and relief. In their search for meaning to life, many turn to everything but God.

There is no spiritual rest apart from a relationship with God, and that relationship must come from receiving Jesus as Saviour.

Invitation to learn (Matt. 11:29-30). Jesus' listeners would have understood His reference to becoming yoked to Him. All of them would have seen a farmer plowing his fields with a pair of oxen yoked together.

A yoke was placed upon a pair of animals to ensure that they would pull together instead of going their separate ways. The implication of Jesus' invitation to the people to take His yoke upon them is very clear. Connected with Jesus, they could be assured of succeeding in life. Jesus' claim "For my yoke is easy, and my burden is light" (Matt. 11:30) must be accepted by faith. After we learn to turn our lives over to His direction, we experience what He said.

Jeremiah 6:16 is a verse that reveals what human nature can be like: "Thus saith the Lord, Stand ye in the ways, and see, and ask for the old paths, where is the good way, and walk therein, and ye shall find rest for your souls. But they said, We will not walk therein."

If they wanted to find rest for their souls, they needed to live by God's ways. He promised them that rest if they did so, but instead of listening to Him, they determined to continue living life the way they wanted. The result was captivity in Babylon. Why are we humans so ignorant and so slow to learn?

—Keith E. Eggert.

QUESTIONS

1. How did Jesus address His Father in this prayer, and what was the tone of His prayer?

2. What contrast did Jesus mention in His prayer, and why is this somewhat unusual?

3. Who are the "wise and prudent" and the "babes" (Matt. 11:25), and what do the latter understand that the others do not?

4. What did Jesus mean by saying all things had been given to Him?

5. How did Jesus say we can know His Father?

6. Why is it important that Jesus was both God and man?

7. Why would the invitation to come and find rest encourage the Jews?

8. What makes this invitation meaningful to today's society?

9. Where did Jesus get the analogy of being yoked with Him, and what is the reason for His invitation?

10. What does Jeremiah 6:16 reveal about human nature?

—Keith E. Eggert.

PRACTICAL POINTS

1. God is not impressed by human wisdom; He delights in one's dependence upon Him (Matt. 11:25).
2. God's delights are not ours; He highly values what we discard and discards what we treasure (vs. 26).
3. Anyone who claims to know God but does not know Jesus Christ as Lord and Saviour is either deceived or a liar (vs. 27).
4. To know Christ is to find relief from the toil of ambition, anxiety, and self-justification (vs. 28).
5. To know Christ we must first know true humility (vs. 29).
6. Christ's yoke is joyously light compared with the endless futility of self-righteousness (vs. 30).

—John M. Lody.

RESEARCH AND DISCUSSION

1. Paul wrote, "Knowledge puffeth up, but charity edifieth" (I Cor. 8:1). Read verses 1-3 and discuss the significance of both knowledge and love within Christ's body.
2. Disappointment is often God's appointment. Share and discuss instances in which God used your disappointment to accomplish His purpose in your life.
3. Today many people are fond of claiming that faith in God does not require believing in Jesus Christ. Discuss the motives behind such a claim and the biblical answers to it.
4. Discuss the meaning of Christ's call to rest in Matthew 11:28-30. What does His rest involve?

—John M. Lody.

Golden Text Illuminated

"Come unto me, all ye that labour and are heavy laden, and I will give you rest" (Matthew 11:28).

The Jews had twisted the purpose of the law. They were looking to the law as a means of salvation rather than as a way of life (Rom. 10:1-3). But the law was intended to show people how to live, not how to be saved (3:20-21).

To compound the problem, the Pharisees had added more rules of conduct to the law of Moses.

The Greek word translated "heavy laden" refers to the fatigue that comes from hard, backbreaking work. The people were worn out from trying to save themselves.

When a person comes to Christ by faith (Heb. 4:9-10), he ceases to work for his salvation and rests in the finished work of Christ.

There are many burdens that people must carry in life, but by far the heaviest burden is the weight of sin. It torments the soul and causes people to fear death (Heb. 2:14-15; 9:27).

The Pharisees offered no relief from the heavy burden of sin. Their message to the people was to keep striving and maybe God would accept them in the end. Jesus' message was to come to Him and rest.

There is no sweeter joy in life than to come to the knowledge that your sins have been put away and that you have been fully accepted by God.

How do we come to the Lord with our heavy burdens? The answer is prayer. The Lord has promised peace of heart to all who bring their needs to God in prayer (Phil. 4:6-7).

—Karl Kloppmann.

Scripture Lesson Text

MATT. 13:54 And when he was come into his own country, he taught them in their synagogue, insomuch that they were astonished, and said, Whence hath this *man* this wisdom, and *these* mighty works?

55 Is not this the carpenter's son? is not his mother called Ma'ry? and his brethren, James, and Jo'ses, and Si'mon, and Ju'das?

56 And his sisters, are they not all with us? Whence then hath this *man* all these things?

57 And they were offended in him. But Je'sus said unto them, A prophet is not without honour, save in his own country, and in his own house.

58 And he did not many mighty works there because of their unbelief.

Revealed in Rejection

Lesson: Matthew 13:54-58

Read: Matthew 13:54-58; Luke 4:16-30

TIME: A.D. 28   PLACE: Nazareth

GOLDEN TEXT — "He did not many mighty works there because of their unbelief" (Matthew 13:58).

Lesson Exposition

REJECTION IN NAZARETH—
Matt. 13:54-56

Jesus teaching at home (Matt. 13:54). Jesus probably had been ministering in Capernaum; so He now left there to return to His hometown of Nazareth.

Apparently, Jesus had visited Nazareth earlier and had spoken in their synagogue (Luke 4:16-21). People were amazed as He spoke.

On this second visit, Jesus again taught. Once again the people who listened were amazed at His teaching. Once again they had the opportunity to listen and believe. On the previous occasion, the people of Nazareth had actually tried to kill Jesus by throwing Him off a cliff (Luke 4:28-30). What would it be like this time? Had they not been hearing about Him and the ministry He and His disciples were having all around Galilee? Would they be proud of one of their own?

It was when He assumed the role of a rabbi that the Jewish people became confused. Rabbinical training was extensive and required many long hours of sitting at the feet of the learned men. Most of that training consisted of passing on traditional interpretations of the

Scriptures, and people knew Jesus had not received such instruction. So how could He consider Himself qualified to teach them?

Examined for credentials (Matt. 13:55-56). What made it particularly hard for the people of Nazareth was being acquainted with Joseph and knowing that he was nothing more than a simple carpenter. By bringing up His father's occupation, the people were regarding Jesus as nothing more than a common laborer.

Mary was still living in Nazareth at that time, and the people mentioned her. That gave no credibility to Jesus as far as being a teacher was concerned, though, because Mary was just the carpenter's wife. His brothers were there and were named in the discussions.

RESTRICTION IN NAZARETH—
Matt. 13:57-58

Jesus explaining their offense (Matt. 13:57). "Jesus' claims caused the people in His hometown to be offended at Him. They stumbled over His words and could not accept them" (Osborne and Comfort, eds., *Life Application Bible Commentary*, Tyndale).

It is an amazing fact that spiritual truth is so offensive to people who are determined to continue in a worldly lifestyle. This kind of reaction to the gospel demonstrates the truth of what the Apostle Paul wrote to the Corinthian church: "But if our gospel be hid, it is hid to them that are lost" (II Cor. 4:3).

Such rejection should cause those of us who believe to be extremely thankful to the Lord for allowing us the privilege of hearing the gospel and having receptive hearts for it. Those who have refused to respond are still going to be accountable to God. According to Romans 1:19, they have an innate knowledge of their need for a relationship with Him. He is also clearly visible in creation (vs. 20); so "they are without excuse."

Jesus had an interesting explanation for His rejection in Nazareth. Jesus said that "a prophet is not without honour, save in his own country, and in his own house" (Matt. 13:57). His own situation proved the statement. While others believed in Him, His own town and family could not.

Jesus restricted in ministry (Matt. 13:58). The people of Nazareth had the omnipotent God in their midst. They needed only to believe, and that could have released the power of God among them in ways they had never conceived of. Matthew had previously indicated the importance of faith in the release of this power.

Matthew 8 describes the desperation of a Roman centurion who had a paralyzed servant (vss. 5-6). Jesus' response honored the belief of the centurion.

It is obvious that Jesus' reticence to do miracles in Nazareth was not because His power was limited. It was simply the lack of faith on the part of His own people.

"This has to be one of the most sorrowful statements in the Bible. Imagine Jesus leaving His hometown, with many people whom He has loved, unable to find the faith that He found in a Gentile centurion (8:13). His own family and close friends were fulfilling Matthew 13:14-15—hearing, but not understanding" (Anders and Weber, *Holman New Testament Commentary*, Broadman & Holman). Surely the lack of understanding and acceptance in Jesus' hometown demonstrates how dark the minds of unbelievers are when it comes to spiritual truth.

—*Keith E. Eggert.*

QUESTIONS

1. Where did Jesus go after Capernaum, and why was this place special to Him?

2. What had happened the previous time He had gone there, and why should it have been better now?

3. What mental hang-up did the people of Nazareth have regarding Jesus teaching in a synagogue?

4. What identity did Jesus have through Joseph?

5. What person living in Nazareth did the people use as a reference?

6. What is known about Jesus' brother James?

7. Why do many people react negatively to the truth?

8. What reason did Jesus give as an explanation for His lack of reception in Nazareth?

9. As a result of Jesus' rejection by the people of Nazareth, what was He unable to do?

10. What had Jesus done previously to show that His inability to do miracles was not due to a loss of power?

—*Keith E. Eggert.*

PRACTICAL POINTS

1. God's own Son taught in small, local assemblies. No venue is too lowly for the preaching of God's Word (Matt. 13:54a).
2. People are often astonished by a familiar figure serving God in an important way (vs. 54b).
3. What becomes overly familiar to people loses value in their estimation (vs. 55a).
4. People often form expectations based on merely vague knowledge of the past (vs. 55b).
5. People often become jealous when someone they have known achieves prominence (vs. 56).
6. Jesus is never surprised by evil responses to Him; all is part of God's plan (vss. 57-58).

—John M. Lody.

RESEARCH AND DISCUSSION

1. Have you ever known people who later became prominent or famous? How did they act toward their former friends? What did their former friends think of them after they had become well-known?
2. The old saying goes "Familiarity breeds contempt." Discuss why this happens and what attitudes contribute to its occurrence. How can we avoid this phenomenon as Christians?
3. Is God ever taken by surprise when people reject Him? Can negative human responses thwart God's purposes? Discuss this topic, founding your arguments on Scripture.

—John M. Lody.

Golden Text Illuminated

"He did not many mighty works there because of their unbelief" (Matthew 13:58).

The people of Nazareth failed to give Jesus the honor He deserved.

As astonished at His powers as they were, they remembered Jesus as just ordinary—no different from themselves. This prevented them from believing in Him.

The rejection that Jesus received from the people of Nazareth surely grieved Him. It would have been like a hometown athlete being booed by the fans. The people He must have felt the closest to rejected Him.

Their unbelief, however, did more than grieve Him. It also prevented Him from doing many mighty works that He desired to do.

There are two possible ways to understand this observation. First, we can understand it to mean that Jesus limited His working to people who exercised faith in Him. The problem with that approach is that there were times when Jesus performed a mighty work when there was no evidence of faith on the part of the recipients of the miracle.

On the other hand, we could understand the above statement to mean that very few people came to Jesus for help because of their unbelief. The rest of Mark 6:5 seems to confirm that this was the case, for it declares, "He could there do no mighty work, save that he laid his hands upon a few sick folk, and healed them." It sounds as if only a few people came to Him.

Let us not keep Christ from working in our lives because we do not seek His help.

—Karl Kloppmann.

Scripture Lesson Text

MATT. 15:21 Then Je'sus went thence, and departed into the coasts of Tyre and Si'don.

22 And, behold, a woman of Ca'naan came out of the same coasts, and cried unto him, saying, Have mercy on me, O Lord, *thou* Son of Da'vid; my daughter is grievously vexed with a devil.

23 But he answered her not a word. And his disciples came and besought him, saying, Send her away; for she crieth after us.

24 But he answered and said, I am not sent but unto the lost sheep of the house of Is'ra-el.

25 Then came she and worshipped him, saying, Lord, help me.

26 But he answered and said, It is not meet to take the children's bread, and to cast *it* to dogs.

27 And she said, Truth, Lord: yet the dogs eat of the crumbs which fall from their masters' table.

28 Then Je'sus answered and said unto her, O woman, great *is* thy faith: be it unto thee even as thou wilt. And her daughter was made whole from that very hour.

Recognized by a Canaanite Woman

Lesson: Matthew 15:21-28

Read: Matthew 15:21-28

TIME: A.D. 29   PLACE: region of Tyre and Sidon

GOLDEN TEXT—"O woman, great is thy faith: be it unto thee even as thou wilt" (Matthew 15:28).

Lesson Exposition

AN UNMET NEED—Matt. 15:21-24

The Canaanite woman's request (Matt. 15:21-22). The last named physical location of Jesus' ministry was Gennesaret (14:34), a small plain located on the northwestern side of the Sea of Galilee. It was apparently from there that Jesus left to go to the Phoenician region of Tyre and Sidon.

Tyre and Sidon were port cities on the Mediterranean Sea in the land of Phoenicia, and both were Canaanite cities. To the Jews, the only people more abhorred than the Canaanites were perhaps the Samaritans.

If He hoped to have some quiet time with His disciples and remain unknown (Mark 7:24), it was not to happen. A Canaanite woman soon recognized Him and appealed to Him for help (Matt. 15:22). Somehow she had heard of His miracle-working power, and when word reached her of His presence, she was not about to let this opportunity get away. Calling Him "Lord, . . . Son of David" shows that she had already recognized Him as the promised Messiah of Israel.

Her problem was not hers alone but more directly her daughter's, who was demon possessed. Jesus had cast out demons (Matt. 9:32-33), and it is possible this woman had heard of it.

The disciples' request (Matt. 15:23-24). A long, antagonistic history lay between Israel and the Canaanites. Perhaps this at least helps explain Jesus' strange action while she cried out to Him. He completely ignored her, which was so contrary to the compassion He consistently showed others.

As Jesus continued to ignore her, she kept pleading until finally His disciples spoke up, asking Him to get rid of her because of her incessant cries. Either they wanted Him to send her away, or their intent may have been for Him to hurry up and do what she asked so that she would leave them alone.

Jesus' response to His disciples makes better sense if we understand that they were asking Him to do what the woman wanted. He said, in essence, "I cannot respond to her that way because I was sent to minister to the lost sheep of Israel—not yet to those who are not part of this nation."

A PRAYER ANSWERED—
Matt. 15:25-28

Jesus' refusal to help (Matt. 15:25-26). Jesus was also giving His disciples a lesson in faith. The next thing we read about this Canaanite woman regards her insistence. She came and worshiped Jesus. Her actions displayed a sense of complete sincerity and devotion. Once again in desperation, she repeated her request. This time it was very simple: "Lord, help me." She knew He was her only hope.

Upon first glance, Jesus' response appears downright cruel. His comment was that it was not proper to take the food prepared for the children of a family and throw it to the dogs instead. The word He used referred to little pet dogs, not the wild, ranging scavengers that were feared and looked down upon by people. His verbal portrait was actually a parable.

The woman immediately understood what He said. It was not a cruel statement but merely an illustration in which the Gentiles were portrayed as not being part of the Jewish family. The children represented Jesus' Jewish family, to whom He was to go first with the message of salvation. The little pet dogs, very much loved by their owners, represented the Gentiles. It was not that Jesus implied the woman was less deserving; she simply did not come first and needed to wait for her time.

Jesus' change of response (Matt. 15:27-28). Since the woman understood the parable, she was not the least bit offended by Jesus' statement. She acknowledged the truth of it when she responded with "Truth, Lord." She was not a "child" in the Jewish family and did not expect to receive what should have gone to them first. She recognized her position as a "dog," but

she was one who was waiting for crumbs to fall her way. Her request was not that any of Israel's blessings be denied them; she wanted only enough to meet her need.

This was exactly the kind of faith Jesus was looking for among His own people. This humble Phoenician woman reached out to Him in belief and simple trust. Is it any wonder that His response displayed His pleasure? After the Canaanite woman expressed her faith, "her daughter was made whole from that very hour" (Matt. 15:28). Because of her recognition of Jesus and belief in who He was and what He could do, she received the desire of her heart.

Do we have the faith that this woman had?

—Keith E. Eggert.

QUESTIONS

1. Where did Jesus go after Gennesaret?
2. Where were Tyre and Sidon?
3. What happened as He hoped for quiet time away from people?
4. How did this woman initially address Jesus, and what was significant about that address?
5. How did Jesus respond to her at first, and what did she do then?
6. Why was Jesus not responding to this Canaanite woman?
7. What was Jesus apparently hoping His disciples would learn?
8. How did Jesus tell her He was not going to answer her request?
9. What was her reply, and what do we learn about her understanding?
10. How did Jesus express His pleasure about her faith?

—Keith E. Eggert.

PRACTICAL POINTS

1. The gospel is meant to go forth to the lost, not to stagnate among believers (Matt. 15:21).
2. God's irresistible grace draws people to Jesus from the ends of the earth (vs. 22).
3. Beware of those who think that some are beyond the reach of God's saving grace (vs. 23).
4. Sometimes we do not understand God's purposes, but we must trust Him anyway (vs. 24).
5. True faith is willing to humble itself without limit to lay hold of Jesus Christ (vss. 25-26).
6. True faith passes God's testing and afterward receives the full rewards of being a child of God (vss. 27-28).
   —John M. Lody.

RESEARCH AND DISCUSSION

1. Discuss the role of the gospel in the life of a believer. List its many uses, both for those who believe and for those who are yet unsaved.
2. Do people seek God, or does God find them? Or does the answer involve both?
3. Do you know people who hold prejudices against certain people or classes of people as being beyond the reach of salvation? Is this attitude even justified, according to the Bible? Support your answers.
4. Share and discuss instances in your life when you had to trust God, although you did not understand His purposes.
5. Discuss the characteristics of true faith.
   —John M. Lody.

Golden Text Illuminated

"O woman, great is thy faith: be it unto thee even as thou wilt" (Matthew 15:28).

As Jesus approached Tyre and Sidon, a woman of Canaan whose daughter was possessed by demons came to meet Him. In great earnestness she pleaded with the Lord to have mercy on her daughter. He said to her, "I am not sent but unto the lost sheep of the house of Israel" (Matt. 15:24) and "It is not meet to take the children's bread, and to cast it to dogs" (vs. 26).

Instead of feeling rejected, the woman saw in this imagery an opportunity to receive blessing. She quickly pointed out that dogs do not go hungry; they eat the crumbs that fall from their master's table.

The Lord credited her with great faith and granted her request.

What was so great about her faith? There are three things that stand out. First, she had absolute confidence that Jesus could heal her daughter.

Often the Lord's people fail to persist in prayer, because they do not have a strong confidence that nothing is too hard for God.

Second, her faith was great because she did not criticize the Lord for hesitating to answer her request. The first words she uttered were "Truth, Lord" (Matt. 15:27). Great faith accepts that the Lord has a good reason for delaying His response.

Third, her faith was great because it revealed a great desire for the answer. Often God delays in order to test how deeply we want what we are asking Him to do. Persistence is fueled by desire.
—Karl Kloppmann.

Scripture Lesson Text

MATT. 16:13 When Je'sus came into the coasts of Caes-a-re'a Phi-lip'pi, he asked his disciples, saying, Whom do men say that I the Son of man am?

14 And they said, Some *say that thou art* John the Bap'tist: some, E-li'as; and others, Jer-e-mi'as, or one of the prophets.

15 He saith unto them, But whom say ye that I am?

16 And Si'mon Pe'ter answered and said, Thou art the Christ, the Son of the living God.

17 And Je'sus answered and said unto him, Blessed art thou, Si'mon Bar–jo'na: for flesh and blood hath not revealed *it* unto thee, but my Father which is in heaven.

18 And I say also unto thee, That thou art Pe'ter, and upon this rock I will build my church; and the gates of hell shall not prevail against it.

19 And I will give unto thee the keys of the kingdom of heaven: and whatsoever thou shalt bind on earth shall be bound in heaven: and whatsoever thou shalt loose on earth shall be loosed in heaven.

20 Then charged he his disciples that they should tell no man that he was Je'sus the Christ.

21 From that time forth began Je'sus to shew unto his disciples, how that he must go unto Je-ru'sa-lem, and suffer many things of the elders and chief priests and scribes, and be killed, and be raised again the third day.

22 Then Pe'ter took him, and began to rebuke him, saying, Be it far from thee, Lord: this shall not be unto thee.

23 But he turned, and said unto Pe'ter, Get thee behind me, Sa'tan: thou art an offense unto me: for thou savourest not the things that be of God, but those that be of men.

24 Then said Je'sus unto his disciples, If any *man* will come after me, let him deny himself, and take up his cross, and follow me.

25 For whosoever will save his life shall lose it: and whosoever will lose his life for my sake shall find it.

26 For what is a man profited, if he shall gain the whole world, and lose his own soul? or what shall a man give in exchange for his soul?

27 For the Son of man shall come in the glory of his Father with his angels; and then he shall reward every man according to his works.

Declared by Peter

Lesson: Matthew 16:13-27

Read: Matthew 16:13-27

TIME: A.D. 29   PLACE: area near Caesarea Philippi

GOLDEN TEXT—"Simon Peter answered and said, Thou art the Christ, the Son of the living God" (Matthew 16:16).

Lesson Exposition

PROBING—Matt. 16:13-16

Jesus' question and the disciples' answer (Matt. 16:13-14). Caesarea Philippi was located approximately twenty-five miles north of the Sea of Galilee at the bottom of the southwest slope of Mount Hermon. It was here that Jesus asked His disciples, "Whom do men say that I the Son of man am?" It was not that Jesus did not already know the answer to that question; it was rather a leading question intended to get the disciples thinking about His deity.

The responses from the disciples included some of the great men in Israel's history. John the Baptist was the first mentioned because he was currently on the minds of many of the people, having recently been killed by Herod. Elijah and Jeremiah were named, along with the idea that He could be one of the other prophets they all knew.

While all those mentioned were honorable men, and in that sense flattering to Jesus, the answers were all wrong. They seemed to point to the general concept that most people considered Jesus to be just another prophet sent from God.

Jesus' follow-up question and Peter's confident response (Matt. 16:15-16). Now Jesus got to the crux of the conversation: "But whom say ye that I am?" What had they learned from all His teaching and healing?

In a characteristically forward manner, Peter responded. He understood that Jesus was the Messiah, the Anointed One. Peter knew that all the Old Testament promises to Israel were being fulfilled in Jesus.

PREPARATION—Matt. 16:17-21

A conferring of blessing and authority (Matt. 16:17-19). Peter's words brought a response of blessing from Jesus, but He also quickly assured him that he could not have come to that conclusion on his own. Jesus' Father in heaven had revealed the truth to him.

When Jesus met Simon Peter, He gave him the name "Cephas," which is the Aramaic word for "rock" (cf. John 1:42). When Jesus said, "Thou art Peter" (Matt. 16:18), He used the Greek word *petros,* also meaning "rock." He then did a play on this word by reminding Peter of his name and saying that on this rock (*petra*) He would build His church. What did He mean? Most likely, He was referring to Peter's statement of faith.

Peter's confession covered the truth of who Christ is and what He had come to fulfill and, as such, is the one foundational truth necessary for the building of the church. Jesus gave assurance that the gates of hell would not destroy it. The Jews would have understood that as a reference to death. Jesus' death would not stop what He had begun.

Explaining Jesus' reference to the keys of the kingdom, J. Dwight Pentecost observed, "The key was a badge of authority . . . to declare salvation to people, and to assure those who believe that they are recipients of eternal life" (*The Words and Works of Jesus Christ,* Zondervan).

A command with some new instruction (Matt. 16:20-21). It seems unusual to us that Jesus would at this point tell His disciples not to tell others that He was the Messiah. He had given plenty of demonstration of who He was and had been rejected by Israel as a whole. He immediately began their preparation by telling them what was coming. We can only imagine the stunned looks on their faces as He spoke.

PRIORITIES—Matt. 16:22-27

The importance of doing the things of God (Matt. 16:22-23). Peter immediately reacted to Jesus' announcement. He was forbidding Jesus to say such things or to allow that such things could even happen! This was the same Peter who had a moment earlier been blessed by Jesus for having a good amount of spiritual insight!

Peter's rebuke brought on a rebuke from Jesus, but it was addressed to the one behind Peter's statement. Satan was trying to get Jesus to avoid the cross; he knew the cross would mean his ultimate, permanent defeat.

The importance of denying self to follow Jesus (Matt. 16:24-25). Pentecost explained, "In order to be a true disciple one must submit himself completely to the will of Jesus Christ. Such a one must deny himself, that is, set aside his own will and his own rights to his own life; he must then submit himself completely to the will of Christ."

The importance of readiness to meet Christ (Matt. 16:26-27). Imagine the horror of being able to obtain everything one's heart desires in life only to awaken after death in torment. It is possible for a believer to be so focused on fulfilling his own desires that he misses out on the joy of the Lord. It is much more costly to not know the Lord at all. Make Jesus Christ the focus of your life. Serve Him with all your heart.

—*Keith E. Eggert.*

QUESTIONS

1. Why was it important for Jesus to question His disciples about who others thought He was?

2. What was the problem with the answers they gave, and what was His personal question to them?

3. What did Peter's answer reveal?

4. What might Jesus have meant by saying He would build His church on the "rock" (Matt. 16:18)?

5. What is the meaning of the "keys" (vs. 19)?

6. What did Jesus command His disciples at this time?

7. How did Peter react to the new information Jesus gave them?

8. How did Jesus respond to Peter, and what did it mean?

9. What does it mean to deny oneself in order to follow Jesus?

10. How did Jesus explain the importance of receiving Him?

—*Keith E. Eggert.*

PRACTICAL POINTS

1. The better one knows Jesus, the more convinced one becomes that He is God (Matt. 16:13-16).
2. Truly knowing Jesus Christ is a special revelation from God the Father (vs. 17).
3. The church of Jesus Christ is built upon the foundation of His apostles' testimony (Matt. 16:18a; cf. Eph. 2:19-21; Rev. 21:14).
4. Christ's church was founded to defeat the very strongholds of hell (Matt. 16:18b-20).
5. Anyone who denies the necessity of Christ's atoning death is serving Satan (vss. 21-23).
6. The road of salvation is paved with self-denial and sacrifice (vss. 24-27).
   — John M. Lody.

RESEARCH AND DISCUSSION

1. Research the biblical proofs for Christ's deity. Good sources are books on Christian apologetics by writers such as Walter Martin and Josh McDowell. These proofs can come in handy when witnessing to unbelievers, especially members of certain cults.
2. Research the history of the formation of the New Testament. Good sources include *The Canon of Scripture* (F. F. Bruce, InterVarsity) and *Inspiration Canonicity of the Bible* (R. Laird Harris, Reformed Academic Press).
3. What does it mean to deny oneself on a daily basis? Research this and discuss it in class.
   — John M. Lody.

Golden Text Illuminated

"Simon Peter answered and said, Thou art the Christ, the Son of the living God" (Matthew 16:16).

The ministry of Jesus made a significant impact on people. Not only did He draw huge crowds, but He also stimulated people to speculate concerning His identity. In light of this discussion, He confronted His disciples with the question "Whom do men say that I the Son of man am?" (Matt. 16:13).

The people held Jesus in high esteem, for they compared Him to the greatest prophets in Israel's history. Their view of Jesus was not high enough, however, for unless they believed that He was who He claimed to be, they would die in their sins (John 8:24).

After hearing what people were saying about Him, Jesus pressed the disciples concerning who they believed He was. Peter quickly fired back, "Thou art the Christ, the Son of the living God." Jesus was moved by Peter's response, for He declared that Peter had not come up with it on His own— "flesh and blood hath not revealed it unto thee" (Matt. 16:17). He knew that this heartfelt confession could have come only from the Father.

As unique as Peter's confession was, it was not the only confession of Christ's true identity (Matt. 21:9; 27:54). However, Scripture does not say that these other confessions were revealed by the Father. Perhaps this indicates that these confessions were not the deep work of the Father but instead were the superficial responses of people who were acting on the impulse of the moment.
— Karl Kloppmann.

Scripture Lesson Text

MATT. 17:1 And after six days Je'sus taketh Pe'ter, James, and John his brother, and bringeth them up into an high mountain apart,

2 And was transfigured before them: and his face did shine as the sun, and his raiment was white as the light.

3 And, behold, there appeared unto them Mo'ses and E-li'as talking with him.

4 Then answered Pe'ter, and said unto Je'sus, Lord, it is good for us to be here: if thou wilt, let us make here three tabernacles; one for thee, and one for Mo'ses, and one for E-li'as.

5 While he yet spake, behold, a bright cloud overshadowed them: and behold a voice out of the cloud, which said, This is my beloved Son, in whom I am well pleased; hear ye him.

6 And when the disciples heard *it,* they fell on their face, and were sore afraid.

7 And Je'sus came and touched them, and said, Arise, and be not afraid.

8 And when they had lifted up their eyes, they saw no man, save Je'sus only.

9 And as they came down from the mountain, Je'sus charged them, saying, Tell the vision to no man, until the Son of man be risen again from the dead.

10 And his disciples asked him, saying, Why then say the scribes that E-li'as must first come?

11 And Je'sus answered and said unto them, E-li'as truly shall first come, and restore all things.

12 But I say unto you, That E-li'as is come already, and they knew him not, but have done unto him whatsoever they listed. Likewise shall also the Son of man suffer of them.

Witnessed by Disciples

Lesson: Matthew 17:1-12

Read: Matthew 17:1-12

TIME: A.D. 29   PLACE: Mount Tabor or Mount Hermon
or Mount Miron

GOLDEN TEXT—"A voice [spoke] out of the cloud, . . . This is my beloved Son, in whom I
am well pleased; hear ye him" (Matthew 17:5).

Lesson Exposition

**SURPRISED DISCIPLES—
Matt. 17:1-4**

**The transfiguration of Jesus (Matt.
17:1-2).** Jesus took Peter, John, and
James upon a mountain to pray. His face
became bright like the sun and His
clothes became gleaming white like light.
The Greek word translated "transfigured" is *metamorphoo,* from which we
get the English word "metamorphosis."

What the disciples were allowed to
see was a preview of the Son of man
coming in His kingdom (Matt. 16:28).
Jesus' appearance is often described
as the outshining of His true glory,
which was of necessity veiled by His
human body of flesh.

**The appearance of Moses and Eli-
jah (Matt. 17:3-4).** Moses and Elijah
were allowed to speak face-to-face
with God.

Moses was the great lawgiver, the
mediator through whom God chose to
give the law to the children of Israel.
Elijah was perhaps the greatest of the
prophets and was used as the symbol
of the forerunner of Jesus, John the
Baptist. They represent both the law
and the prophets, the entire Old Testa-

ment Scriptures (Matt. 7:12; 22:40).

The disciples saw the three men
talking together. Peter's suggestion
that three tabernacles be made
sounds typical of him, for he regularly
said things without thinking everything
through.

FEARFUL DISCIPLES—Matt. 17:5-8

**A voice from the cloud (Matt. 17:5-
6).** Peter's offer was interrupted when
they were suddenly overshadowed by
a bright cloud. God Himself came and
assured them that Jesus truly was His
Son and that He was very pleased with
Him. They should therefore be very at-
tentive to Him.

The verbal proclamation from God
was the same as at Jesus' baptism
(Matt. 3:17), but the addition of the
words "hear ye him" (17:5) immediately elevated Jesus above Moses and
Elijah. The whole scene caused great
fear in the disciples, and they fell on
their faces before God.

**The reassurance for the disciples
(Matt. 17:7-8).** Jesus had often spoken
to the disciples about His Father, and
now suddenly they heard His voice. No
wonder they were so terrified. Jesus

understood their agitation; He came and touched them, telling them their fears were unfounded.

After Jesus spoke, the disciples lifted their heads and looked, only to discover that Jesus stood there alone. Moses, Elijah, and the cloud were gone. Everything had returned to "normal."

CURIOUS DISCIPLES—
Matt. 17:9-12

The question about Elijah (Matt. 17:9-10). Jesus told the disciples not to tell anyone what they had seen until after His resurrection. There were probably several reasons for this. First, no one who had not been present would be able to understand. Second, if they were to tell what they had seen, too much attention would be given to them instead of to Jesus.

Third, the leaders of Israel had already rejected Jesus as their Messiah, and He did not intend to promote Himself further. Fourth, those who did believe Jesus was the promised Messiah would want once again to make Him king if they heard of this incident.

Apparently one of the reasons the religious leaders rejected Jesus was the lack of an appearance by Elijah. They were probably basing their teaching on Malachi 4:5. But now the three had seen Elijah; so they wondered how that appearance fit into these teachings.

The explanation about Elijah (Matt. 17:11-12). Jesus assured them that it was true. Elijah would come first to restore all things. He then said, "But I say unto you, That Elias is come already, and they knew him not, but have done unto him whatsoever they listed."

In Matthew 11, Jesus gave an explanation about John (vss. 10-14). John was an Elijah-like figure who ministered in ways similar to the Old Testament Elijah. According to Jesus, he fulfilled the Malachi 4:5 prophecy. Now

that the leaders had rejected John and refused to accept Jesus as their Messiah, He would not set up His kingdom. It was in God's plan, of course, for Him to suffer and pay the price for sin.

There is, therefore, a future fulfillment that will come prior to "the great and dreadful day of the Lord" (Mal. 4:5), a reference to the judgment that is coming. Another Elijah-like figure will appear (cf. Rev. 11:1-10).

Peter, James, and John glimpsed the glorified Jesus. His own Father affirmed that He is His Son. Strong testimony like that should remove any doubts about Him.

—Keith E. Eggert.

QUESTIONS

1. How many disciples did Jesus take with Him up the mountain, and what did they see?
2. What was revealed to them about Jesus in this incident?
3. Why was Jesus' glory normally hidden?
4. What did Moses and Elijah have in common?
5. What is a likely reason Moses and Elijah were sent to be with Jesus on this occasion?
6. What did Peter offer to do, what interrupted his offer, and what was the disciples' response?
7. Who spoke from the cloud, and what was the message?
8. How did Jesus allay the fear of the disciples?
9. What command did Jesus give the disciples prior to their return, and why did He say this?
10. What do we know about Malachi's prophecy about Elijah?

—Keith E. Eggert.

PRACTICAL POINTS

1. God chooses some people for special experiences that others will not have (Matt. 17:1).
2. Jesus Christ is the full personification of God's glory; to know Him is to know God (vs. 2).
3. We must never elevate any mere human to the level of Christ's authority (vss. 3-5).
4. When we are stricken with fears, Jesus alone can offer us true comfort (vss. 6-8).
5. Some experiences with God must remain private until the right time comes (vs. 9).
6. Some think they are ready for Christ's coming, but they will be surprised by how unprepared they really are (vss. 10-12).

—*John M. Lody.*

RESEARCH AND DISCUSSION

1. Research people throughout the Bible who were special to God (for example, Noah, Moses, David, Elijah, Elisha, John, Paul, and so forth). Which characteristics do they share? Which ones make them different? What can we learn from them about God's value system?
2. Some Christians seem to admire prominent figures from Christian history more than others. Discuss the propriety of dedicating places, organizations, or buildings to persons other than Jesus Christ. Is this a good practice? Why or why not?
3. Discuss what it means to be ready for Jesus' coming. Are you ready? How can we be ready?

—*John M. Lody.*

Golden Text Illuminated

"A voice [spoke] out of the cloud, . . . This is my beloved Son, in whom I am well pleased; hear ye him" (Matthew 17:5).

Jesus' transfiguration was a preview of Him coming in His kingdom. Peter was greatly moved by what he saw and offered to make three shelters—one for Jesus, one for Moses, and one for Elijah. Peter was most likely thinking of the Feast of Tabernacles, which required the people to live in booths to remember their experience of leaving Egypt.

Peter's good intentions were marred by his attempt to place Jesus on the same level as Moses and Elijah. The Father quickly corrected Peter by overshadowing the disciples in a bright cloud (cf. Exod. 40:34-35) and speaking to them out of the cloud, saying, "This is my beloved Son, in whom I am well pleased; hear ye him."

When the disciples heard the voice of God, they were terrified and fell on their faces. Jesus came to them and touched them and said, "Arise, and be not afraid" (Matt. 17:7).

Peter never forgot this cherished moment. In II Peter 1:16-19 he recalled the event, specifically mentioning that he had been an eyewitness of the majesty of the Lord (His glorious transfiguration) and had heard the voice of God affirming that Jesus was His beloved Son.

The disciples had learned in a dramatic way that Jesus was not just another great prophet. He was greater than Moses or Elijah; He was the divine Son of God, who fully pleased the Father. They owed Him their undivided attention and complete obedience.

—*Karl Kloppmann.*

Scripture Lesson Text

MATT. 26:6 Now when Je′sus was in Beth′a-ny, in the house of Si′mon the leper,

7 There came unto him a woman having an alabaster box of very precious ointment, and poured it on his head, as he sat *at meat.*

8 But when his disciples saw *it,* they had indignation, saying, To what purpose *is* this waste?

9 For this ointment might have been sold for much, and given to the poor.

10 When Je′sus understood *it,* he said unto them, Why trouble ye the woman? for she hath wrought a good work upon me.

11 For ye have the poor always with you; but me ye have not always.

12 For in that she hath poured this ointment on my body, she did *it* for my burial.

13 Verily I say unto you, Wheresoever this gospel shall be preached in the whole world, *there* **shall also this, that this woman hath done, be told for a memorial of her.**

Anointed by a Woman in Bethany

Lesson: Matthew 26:6-13

Read: Matthew 26:6-13

TIME: A.D. 30   PLACE: Bethany

GOLDEN TEXT — "In that she hath poured this ointment on my body, she did it for my burial" (Matthew 26:12).

Lesson Exposition

SOMETHING VIEWED AS A WASTE — Matt. 26:6-9

Adoration (Matt. 26:6-7). Jesus was now in Bethany, a village on the southeastern slope of the Mount of Olives on the road going from Jerusalem to Jericho. There are several places in the Gospels where we read of Jesus' connection with this village, but three events stand out.

Bethany was the home of Lazarus, Mary, and Martha and was therefore where Lazarus was raised from death (John 11). Jesus liked to retreat there. Bethany was also the place where Jesus took His disciples when He was about to ascend back to heaven (Luke 24:50-51).

This week's lesson text looks at another significant incident in Bethany. Apparently, Jesus spent the nights in Bethany during this last week of His life, and on this particular occasion, He was in the house of Simon the leper. Simon was probably one of those who had been healed by Jesus, and he had evidently invited Him in for supper (John 12:2). Jesus was sitting at the

table — or, more accurately, reclining on a cushion in the common posture for eating. John also recorded that Martha served and Lazarus was there.

A woman came in with an alabaster box of ointment. John identified her as Mary (John 12:3). The first two Gospels say she poured the ointment over His head, and John says it was over His feet. That would lead us to believe she did both. This was a very costly ointment.

Indignation (Matt. 26:8-9). The value of the ointment prompted the reaction of Jesus' disciples. They became indignant. John points out Judas as the primary critic (12:4), emphasizing that he knew the exact value of the ointment and that his motivation was selfish. In the view of the critics, this use of such a costly ointment was a waste. It could have been sold for a good price and the money used to benefit poor people.

"Mary's gift to Jesus was worth a year's wages. Perfume such as this was used in burial rites because embalming was not the Jewish custom. Perfume covered the odor of the dead body"

(Osborne and Comfort, eds., *Life Application Bible Commentary,* Tyndale).

Mary was able to recognize who was present at the table that day, while the disciples were still deficient in their understanding. Her act was one of deep devotion and worship. Their attitude was one of doubt and criticism.

SOMETHING VIEWED AS A MEMORIAL — Matt. 26:10-13

Admonition (Matt. 26:10-11). Jesus reprimanded His disciples for their attitude. In doing so, He expressed approval for Mary and her actions. They must have said something to her, because when Jesus spoke to them, His first words were "Why trouble ye the woman?" In other words, they were to leave her alone. What she had done was a good thing, and it had been done for Him, not for anyone else. Her focus on Him was admirable.

When Jesus said, "For ye have the poor always with you; but me ye have not always" (Matt. 26:11), He was not in any way implying that those who were poor were unimportant to Him. What He was saying was that His time with them was now becoming very short and their opportunities to be with Him and minister to Him would soon be gone. The poor, on the other hand, would still be there, and they would have continued opportunities to minister to them.

Explanation (Matt. 26:12-13). Mary had always had a love for Jesus and His teaching. In Luke 10:38-42 we read that when Jesus was in their home one day, Martha rushed around getting lunch ready while Mary sat in front of Jesus and listened to His teaching. Martha complained to Jesus, asking Him to tell Mary to help her. Jesus said Mary was doing the better thing in listening to His teaching.

Mary also serves as an example of being focused on the Lord. She had again demonstrated that focus in

anointing her Lord. Jesus said her action was an anointing for His burial. Whether she did it with that in mind is not known. She might have been simply expressing her love and devotion.

On the other hand, maybe Mary was thinking of His coming death because He had spoken of it often. The disciples did not seem to grasp the meaning of His statements, but maybe Mary did. The preaching of the gospel throughout the world would include her act of devotion as an example of what Jesus wants from all those who follow Him and claim Him as Saviour.

—Keith E. Eggert.

QUESTIONS

1. Where was Bethany, and why do we think Jesus went there regularly?
2. What events made Bethany a special place in Jesus' ministry?
3. Who was hosting Jesus at this time, and who else was present?
4. What occurred that caught everyone's attention, and what was the reaction of the disciples?
5. How much in terms of salary was the ointment worth?
6. In doing what she did, what did Mary seem to understand better than everyone else who was there?
7. What did Jesus say first when He became aware of what was being said about Mary by those present?
8. How did Jesus answer their concern about selling the ointment and using the money for the poor?
9. How does Mary serve as an example for believers today?
10. Why was a contrast of ideas evident in the house of Simon the leper that day?

—Keith E. Eggert.

PRACTICAL POINTS

1. Love and faith lead some to perform extraordinary acts of devotion that serve as examples for us all (Matt. 26:6-7).
2. Whenever good is done, there will be the jealous, the critical, and the joyful (vs. 8).
3. Some pretend to think of the poor while their hearts are really selfish (vs. 9).
4. He who is idle should not find fault with one who serves feebly but the best that he can (vs. 10).
5. Mere human effort and wisdom can never eradicate any of the evils of our fallen world (vs. 11).
6. Enduring greatness is found in a life sacrificed wholly in love for Jesus Christ (vss. 12-13).

—John M. Lody.

RESEARCH AND DISCUSSION

1. Have you ever been criticized for doing something good? Discuss why people so often seem reluctant to give proper credit to those who sincerely strive to do good. What factors can sometimes spoil good intentions?
2. Since Jesus has already told us that the poor will always be with us, why should we as Christians bother meeting people's physical needs? Discuss the biblical view of charitable works.
3. Besides the woman with the precious ointment, research and discuss other marginal characters who have found a lasting place in the Gospels.

—John M. Lody.

Golden Text Illuminated

"In that she hath poured this ointment on my body, she did it for my burial" (Matthew 26:12).

Jesus was in Bethany toward the end of His ministry. While there He had a meal in the house of Simon the leper. During the meal, Mary, the sister of Lazarus, took a jar of precious ointment and poured it on Jesus' head and feet (Matt. 26:6-7; John 12:1-3).

When the disciples saw the costliness of her gift, they were irate. They wanted to know why she had not sold the ointment and given the proceeds to the poor.

Instead of rebuking this woman, Jesus commended her for having the foresight to anoint His body for burial in advance (Matt. 26:12).

Even though the disciples did take the Lord's repeated words concerning His rapidly approaching death seriously, Mary of Bethany took them very seriously. She believed that when Jesus said something, He meant it! He was soon going to die in Jerusalem, and this was the only clear opportunity to honor Him by anointing His body for burial.

We also need to recognize special opportunities to honor and serve our Lord. There are many opportunities that are continually present, such as giving to the poor. However, other opportunities are here today but gone tomorrow, as was the opportunity to anoint the body of Jesus for burial.

That this was her true motivation can be seen in the tremendous praise that the Lord heaped upon her. Wherever the gospel is preached throughout the world, this woman's act of devotion to Christ will also be proclaimed.

—Karl Kloppmann.

PARAGRAPHS ON PLACES AND PEOPLE

RAMA

Ramah, an Old Testament city located north of Jerusalem, was a stop for travelers going north to Beth–el. It is spelled "Rama" in Matthew.

Because of its location between Israel and Judah, Ramah could represent both kingdoms. Foreign conquerors assembled the defeated people of Israel and Judah there and then deported them to faraway places. Jeremiah 31:15, concerning a tragedy in Ramah, is quoted in Matthew 2:18. In this prophecy, Ramah and Rachel are compared symbolically. Rachel could represent the kingdoms of both Israel and Judah since she was the grandmother of Ephraim (another name for Israel) and the mother of Benjamin (the tribes of Benjamin and Judah made up the kingdom of Judah).

Rachel, long dead, is pictured in Jeremiah 31:15 as weeping for the conquered people herded to Ramah and sent into exile. The parallel verse in Matthew depicts Rachel weeping once more, this time for the slaughter of Bethlehem's infants.

PINNACLE OF THE TEMPLE

There is much speculation about the location of the "pinnacle of the temple" (Matt. 4:5). Scholars tend to consider that Satan took Jesus to a point where the fall would have been the farthest.

Possibly, that place was the edge of the roof of Herod's royal porch. Located on the eastern side of the temple, it overlooked the Kidron Valley some 450 feet below. The historian Josephus wrote that the valley floor was not visible from the porch.

ARCHELAUS

Archelaus was born around 22 B.C. to Herod the Great and his wife Malthace. He inherited a third part of Herod's kingdom (Judea, Samaria, and Idumea) and began to govern in 4 B.C.

Mediocrity and brutality marked Archelaus's reign. The killing of three thousand people at Passover and widespread Jewish revolt gave a bad start to his reign. He removed a Jewish high priest he believed had supported rebels and installed one favorable to him.

It was fear of Archelaus and God's warning that caused Joseph, Mary, and Jesus not to return to Judea. God sent them to Nazareth for their safety and to fulfill Scripture.

Political and family strife brought an end to Archelaus's reign. A delegation of Jews and Samaritans complained to Augustus about his cruelty. His brothers went to Rome and brought charges of ineptitude against him. In A.D. 6, Archelaus was banished to Gaul.

NAASSON

The name "Naasson" in Matthew 1:4 is the Greek form of the Hebrew name "Nahshon," meaning "enchanter" or "little serpent."

Nahshon was a leader of the tribe of Judah (Num. 2:3). Judah was first to proceed as Israel marched through the desert, and Nahshon led the way (2:3; 7:12-17). His sister Elisheba married Aaron (Exod. 6:23). He assisted Moses in taking a census of Israel (Num. 1:7). At the dedication of the tabernacle, he was the first to present his offering (7:12-17). Nahshon's lineage included Boaz, Obed, Jesse, David, and Jesus Christ, our Lord.

—Don Ruff.

Daily Bible Readings for Home Study and Worship

(Readings are for the week previous to the lesson topics.)

1. 6 December. The Lineage of David

M.—I Have Been with You. II Sam. 7:8-11.
T.—I Will Establish Forever. II Sam. 7:12-17.
W.—David's Response to God. II Sam. 7:18-22.
T.—God's Name Magnified Forever. II Sam. 7:23-26.
F.—The Lord Sits Enthroned. Ps. 9:7-11.
S.—Steadfast Love to His Anointed. Ps. 18:43-50.
S.—Jesus, Son of David. Ruth 4:13-17; Matt. 1:1-6.

2. 13 December. The Foreshadowing of Messiah's Birth

M.—A Ruler from Bethlehem. Mic. 5:1-5.
T.—I Sent You Prophets. Matt. 23:29-39.
W.—Preparing the Way. Mark 1:1-8.
T.—The Lord Is with You. Luke 1:26-29.
F.—What Prophets Desired to See. Luke 10:21-24.
S.—Prophets from of Old. Luke 1:68-75.
S.—The Promise Fulfilled. Isa. 7:13-17; Luke 1:30-38.

3. 20 December. Emmanuel's Birth (Christmas)

M.—The Fullness of Time. Gal. 4:1-7.
T.—God with Me Wherever I Go. Gen. 35:1-4.
W.—May God Not Leave Us. I Kings 8:54-61.
T.—God Ahead of Us. II Chron. 13:10-15.
F.—A Greater One with Us. II Chron. 32:1-8.
S.—God Is with Us. Isa. 8:5-10.
S.—Jesus, Emmanuel. Matt. 1:18-25.

4. 27 December. Confirming Messiah's Birth

M.—The Beginning of Wisdom. Prov. 9:7-12.
T.—Give Me Wisdom. II Chron. 1:7-12.
W.—Gaining a Wise Heart. Ps. 90:11-17.
T.—Those Who Find Wisdom. Prov. 3:13-23.
F.—Where Is the Child? Matt. 2:1-6.
S.—Overwhelmed with Joy. Matt. 2:10-15.
S.—Finding and Protecting Jesus. Matt. 2:7-9, 16-23.

5. 3 January. Proclaimed in Baptism

M.—The Origin of John's Baptism. Matt. 21:23-27.
T.—John, More than a Prophet. Luke 7:24-30.
W.—John's Testimony of Jesus. John 1:24-34.
T.—Calling on the Name of Jesus. Rom. 10:8-17.
F.—The Necessity of Repentance. Matt. 3:7-10.
S.—Buried and Raised with Christ. Rom. 6:1-11.
S.—Jesus Baptized by John. Matt. 3:1-6, 11-17.

6. 10 January. Strengthened in Temptation

M.—Enduring Trials and Temptations. Jas. 1:12-16.
T.—Times of Testing. Luke 8:5-8, 11-15.
W.—Restore Others but Take Care. Gal. 6:1-5.
T.—Stay Awake and Pray. Matt. 26:36-46.
F.—The Way to Pray. Matt. 6:9-15.
S.—Our Temptation and God's Faithfulness. I Cor. 10:6-13.
S.—Jesus' Victory over Temptation. Matt. 4:1-11.

7. 17 January. Demonstrated in Acts of Healing

M.—A Physician Needed. Luke 5:27-32.
T.—A Cry for Healing. Ps. 107:17-22.

W.—A Prayer for Healing. II Kings 20:1-7.
T.—An Amazing Faith. Matt. 8:5-13.
F.—The Father's Loving Care. Hos. 11:1-4.
S.—Sent Out to Heal. Matt. 10:1-8.
S.—Jesus' Healing Ministry. Matt. 9:27-34; 11:2-6.

8. 24 January. Declared in Prayer

M.—A Listening Father. John 11:38-44.
T.—Whenever You Pray. Matt. 6:5-8.
W.—Praying Alone. Matt. 14:22-33.
T.—Prayer and Blessing on Children. Matt. 19:13-15.
F.—Pray for Your Persecutors. Matt. 5:43-48.
S.—Prayer and Faith. Matt. 21:18-22.
S.—The Father's Gracious Will. Matt. 11:25-30.

9. 31 January. Revealed in Rejection

M.—A Man of Suffering. Isa. 53:1-9.
T.—No Knowledge of God. Hos. 4:1-6.
W.—Rejecting God's Command. Mark 7:5-13.
T.—The Lord Disciplines Those He Loves. Prov. 3:5-12.
F.—Is Not This Joseph's Son? Luke 4:16-22.
S.—Rejected at Home. Luke 4:23-30.
S.—No Honor in Unbelief. Matt. 13:54-58.

10. 7 February. Recognized by a Canaanite Woman

M.—Revelation to the Gentiles. Luke 2:25-35.
T.—God Shows No Partiality. Rom. 2:1-11.
W.—A Light for the Gentiles. Acts 13:44-49.
T.—Nations Come to Your Light. Isa. 60:1-5.
F.—Nations Walk by God's Light. Rev. 21:22-27.
S.—In Him the Gentiles Hope. Rom. 15:7-13.
S.—Great Is Your Faith! Matt. 15:21-28.

11. 14 February. Declared by Peter

M.—My Sheep Hear My Voice. John 10:22-30.
T.—Believe in the Good News. Mark 1:9-15.
W.—Sheep Without a Shepherd. Mark 6:34-44.
T.—Help My Unbelief. Mark 9:14-27.
F.—Ask and Believe. Mark 11:20-25.
S.—Both Lord and Messiah. Acts 2:29-36.
S.—You Are the Messiah. Matt. 16:13-27.

12. 21 February. Witnessed by Disciples

M.—Eyewitnesses of Jesus' Majesty. II Pet. 1:16-21.
T.—Witness of the True Light. John 1:6-13.
W.—The Kingdom Has Come. Matt. 12:22-28.
T.—Compassion from the Son of David. Matt. 20:29-34.
F.—Hailed as the Son of David. Matt. 21:1-11.
S.—To This We Are Witnesses. Acts 3:11-16.
S.—Listen to Him. Matt. 17:1-12.

13. 28 February. Anointed by a Woman in Bethany

M.—Give Liberally. Deut. 15:7-11.
T.—Women Devoted to Prayer. Acts 1:12-14.
W.—Women Facing Persecution. Acts 8:1-3; 9:1-2.
T.—Women Believers Baptized. Acts 16:12-22.
F.—Leading Women Accept Christ. Acts 17:1-4.
S.—A Hospitable Woman. Acts 16:11-15.
S.—A Good Service for Jesus. Matt. 26:6-13.